The Answer to Cancer:
A Simple Solution for the Western Condition

Ted Whidden
www.TheBrainCan. com
P. O. Box 158
Chipley, Florida, USA 32428
TedWhidden@gmail.com

Joseph A. "Doc" Mathea

and

Theodore L. (Ted) Whidden

The Answer to Cancer:
A Simple Solution for the Western Condition

Authored by:
Joseph A. "Doc" Mathea and
Theodore L. (Ted) Whidden

Publisher:
Ponder the Papyrus Publishing
Chipley, Florida

ISBN: 9780996747127

Forward by Ted Whidden

I am glad to see that Doc Mathea is releasing inventions and approaches to thwart the modern medical situations of people. In seeing his lab I have viewed dozens of inventions and approaches that will address complicated illnesses simply.

I see Doctor Mathea's work as literally the most significant example of a person turning over the tables of the money changers. With the shocking originality and inventiveness of Nikolai Tesla and the forward thinking of Einstein, Doc is plowing new ground using simple science. Healing breast cancer, autism, birth defects, while treating advanced HIV/AIDS and cancer, and so many other sicknesses appear so easy with his approach.

How the "health" community has missed and obscured the obvious for so long boggles the mind. The unveiling of these simple laws of nature opens the door for Doc Mathea's work, uncovering health conspiracy hidden in the earth.

By addressing a form of chaos theory in the body and unraveling the seemingly complicated patterns of health, Doc Mathea may have developed what appears a silver bullet to cure all sickness. His body reconciliation approach which he named after me seems to eradicate a vast majority of conditions required for sickness to exist. I was his first "guinea pig" in a way, and he cast the sickness out of this pig!

The secrets released in this first book in a series if/when employed will likely reduce 60% of all cancers in the short run (reducing them in both mass and count). It will likely reduce all other sickness in the short run by 40%. Over the long haul this book series will lead to the eradication of issues surrounding HIV/Aids, autism, cancer, kidney/liver issues, brain/concussion issues, and will lead to multiplied health and wealth benefits by the nations and regions that embrace the approach.

Mathea represents a veritable super-hero for humanity in a declining world. He shows that saving mankind is more honorable than prof-iteering. I celebrated a personal resurrection of life when I turned my care over to the only person who appeared to have the answers to save me. Doctor Mathea, I salute you.

I asked Doc one time how he knew what he knew. His response was simple and complete. He said, "I pray, son. I pray."

God has not only blessed Doc, but in turn he blesses countless thou-sands (someday millions) with the simple cure for things once thought complicated. God gave him keys, and he is willing to give them away in this book. I hope that Doc continues to pray and I pray that he continues to show the absolute, undeniable power and presence of the One he prays to for all who read. To God be the glory for this care-taker of the Body.

INDEX

CHAPTER One

In the Beginning

The disaster described within this book gives rise to a series of health questions and thus eventually solutions. These discoveries seem to have nearly universal application in reconciling the physical health of persons who have compromised health. The loss of the immune system forced a victim/patient to search for common denominators in their sickness. By identifying, attacking and removing common denominators to sicknesses health is restored through a "silver bullet solution". There are common components to virtually every sickness on earth. Once you remove those common denominators/components amazing breakthroughs in health take place very quickly. The general and specific wellness produced opens new reserves for the body to address all sickness. It is much like a tune up for your immune system. The approach outlined will help to address every sickness mentioned in this book, and many that are not. ("The Chemical Conspiracy" will address more applications to this approach.) The combined approaches outlined will in many ways outdate (and out produce) any and all health systems presently employed. Simple can be powerful with just a little education. Imbalance in education often results in weakness on one side. This series of books will serve to restore balance and expose frailties in current systems and approaches. These simple approaches are available to all mankind, yet prior to now the secrets are not being shared. Focal to this presentation is a release that was accurate 1000 years ago and it will be accurate 1000 years from now. For some reason no one has shared it sufficiently. The point of this book is to share a nearly universal approach to wellness that has helped many walk away from the bondage of sickness. The situation that initiated this most amazingly simple yet powerful discovery requires introduction.

The main subject or "guinea pig" for the study was leading an exceptional life. Health, wealth, exotic travel, adventure, and more were in the palm of the hand of Ted Whidden. In June/July of 2010, Whidden was the insurance representative on the deck of the drilling ship that capped the "Deepwater Horizon" (Macondo) BP Oil Spill in the U.S. Gulf of Mexico, the largest man initiated natural disaster to the environment possibly in history and this was the guy the London Insurance market (Lloyd's of London) had on the scene to witness and report the on scene events on behalf of world financial market; leading to completion of the capping of the well. Fortunately, that project completed in July 2010. Whidden, at the peak of his career, seemed to have everything going for him. A couple of other edgy assignments followed.

One month after the capping of the Deepwater Horizon Well, Whidden's phone rang. It was a personal phone call from someone in a broken down Porsche some 6 hours from home. Whidden advised that after he got some sleep he would grab a truck/SUV from the farm, connect a trailer and come get the stranded friend and their vehicle. What began as a "good Samaritan" effort to assist someone in need would end up wrecking Whidden's world, and crushing the hopes, dreams, and resources of a once successful entrepreneur/consultant.

All was in order rolling along Interstate 10 in Northwest Florida while returning with the broken down Porsche. While heading west in Suwannee County, Florida near Live Oak, in an instant all hell broke loose, literally. While easing along the road, squared up in their own lane, at about midnight on August 29, 2010 Whidden's trailer/cargo was struck from behind (rear end collision) by a high speed 18 wheeler.

Evidence indicates the 18 wheeler had some form of cruise control engaged, as the 18 wheeler increased power to overcome the power loss as a result of the initial contact. The 18 wheeler operator was either not aware of the collision, or was aware and had not reacted yet. The nylon straps holding the

Porsche began to stretch and one at the time break thus allowing the Porsche to be pushed through the back window of Whidden's SUV.

In one perspective this was a perfect accident because the numerous nylon straps released the Porsche squarely through the back window of the SUV, and the 18 wheeler kept coming. The 18 wheeler road up on the back of Whidden's trailer and continued increasing power. Apparently due to the over speed of the engine on the 18 wheeler and the strange lights shining up into the sky in front of the 18 wheeler the trucker awoke realizing something was wrong. The 18 wheeler operator locked up his brakes a full 250 feet or so after point of impact, thus Whidden's SUV and trailer rig was accelerated from 50-55 mph to 100 mph in less than 250 feet.

When the 18 wheeler hit his brakes the two trailer rigs began to disconnect, yet this left Whidden's truck/SUV, trailer and cargo at an uncontrolled 100 mph speed. Whidden's vehicles careened down the road for an estimated 1100 feet before coming to a crash stop.

At the scene of final stopping Whidden's vehicle was crushed from behind with ripples of steel across the top from where the frame/chassis bent, the Porsche was stuck in the back window. The SUV doors were jammed shut and the seat backs broke. All the tools, ramps, etc. in the SUV were shifted forward at the time of the crash stop. Whidden was draped over the steering wheel with all the tools, ramps, etc. piled on top of him.

At one moment prior to the accident all was perfect in Whidden's world, then in an instant it was all taken away. Problem is that what is good in this world, and what is bad in this world are not always apparent. Whidden felt prior to the accident that all was well, but this may not have been true. Whidden thought that following the wreck and surviving meant all was well, but this may not have been true. The problem with life is perceptions are not always true. Many people are sick now, or soon will be and they may not have the ability to properly gauge, understand or correct their situation. The medical community are disadvantaged for a number of reasons. The common medical approach will often lead a person in the wrong direction. Whidden would find great disappointments in the medical approach and the lack of understanding to follow in the coming months/years. This book is presented to help others learn an approach to shock/trauma as well as loss of immunity and a host of sicknesses to produce health.

As the days following the wreck passed Whidden awoke with bruises on his face showing his face hit the steering wheel. He had bodily stiffness, inflammation and a host of bruising and issues manifested. Internal issues became apparent. Whidden seemed to have an elevated adrenaline/excitement for weeks, will an irregular speech impediment. Medical personnel advised this should pass with time. Meanwhile, what developed was Whidden's hyper adrenaline exhausted his body's resources of this chemical, then cortisol (the fight or flight/stress hormone) took over and effectively shut down Whidden's immune system intermittently over the next 2 years more or less. Imagine going through life without an immune system. How long would you live? What would kill you and when and how? The steps to learning how to cope will help others boost their immune system dramatically. (This approach should prove important for HIV/Aids patients and all others with sickness and/or immune disorders.)

The hyper cortisol situation within Whidden's body took over control of the body and immune system. As you study cortisol you will find it is the hormone that gives you the shakes and cold sweats following any near-miss traffic situation. Have you ever had a dog run out in front of you, then you swerve to miss it? As you move down the road some 5-20 minutes later you get rattled, shaky, and get cold sweats? Well, that was from a nanosecond dose of cortisol. Meanwhile, Whidden's system gave him high doses of cortisol for months. This was not only late and improperly diagnosed by medical providers, it was not properly treated. It was allowed to run rampant through his system causing a host of problems.

Have you ever seen or heard of someone indelibly changed

from a traumatic event? Often something happens and they subsequently die of "unrelated causes" somewhere a few months later. These issues are often DIRECTLY RELATED to the trauma and a cascade effect of issues that happen to the victim of a traumatic accident. Rarely are they properly treated. Whidden's survival was rare. The experiences are being shared to save others. Often financial interests in a traumatic event stall their actions in anticipation the patient/victim will die from "unrelated events" thus they avoid payment. It is a sick system. There are at times more people working against the sick person than are working to help them.

What developed with Whidden was a loss of normal immune system function for more than 2 years. As a result Whidden had to learn how to fight as much sickness as possible without an immune system. Oh, by the way, he did it to a large extent without drugs or chemicals. The system is so simple and effective that no one wants you to know, because it will work very cheaply and efficiently with virtually no use of drugs and conventional medicine. It works very well in conjunction with modern medicine, but makes modern medicine work so much more efficiently. You must understand there are forces that do not want you to know, understand and follow a simple, cheap, universal system for cleaning up the human body and preparing for health. The system and the science needed to sustain and ultimately heal or maintain Whidden's body will likely work for you and others. It is too simple to fail, yet so simple and cheap that medical providers and large pharmaceutical companies can't make big money on a simple, natural, bullet proof system. (Pick up the phone and call your sick friends and family. Tell them you have their answer.)

If you understand the dark road ahead of Whidden, you may see your condition is not nearly as desperate, but Whidden himself did not see the need for this approach prior to his accident. If he had done this prior to the accident as a system for maintaining health he may have recovered faster and better, and may not have suffered as long. There is no way to know for sure.

The system could help you with virtually any and all conditions of the body. It is almost too simple to fail. The only way to failure for most is failing to follow instructions, or trying to "modify" or amplify the results without full understanding. It simply works as it is put forward, and should eradicate many sicknesses in the body.

Bless you and yours in your health pursuit. Details in a refined version follow, with results that can be anticipated. As a result of actual damages including brain damage and concussion issues Whidden now uses a form of this approach to maintain wellness. It has been overwhelmingly effective, yet due to a recurring environmental effect Whidden has had to repeat this process over and over. A refined approach to wellness needed to be shared. Here is your key to health in the following chapters.

CHAPTER Two

Loss of Immune System

In the event that you ever find yourself with a compromised immune system, an auto-immune disorder, or without an immune system, there are a few very simple things you must understand. If your system is not so compromised, the same simple systems still apply. The key is that if you are dying, you will often keep dying until you start living. The body is always either improving its condition, or the condition is deteriorating. It does not stay at one level very long. What many find after a traumatic event is that there are/were things lurking in their system ready to take them down when the system faltered. A classic example is the immunization shots you have taken over your lifetime. Immunization shots imbed sickness in your system, in theory, at a time when your body can handle/manage the sickness. When your system is compromised, many things are waiting to rise up. Thus following a traumatic event one's system appears to deteriorate from "unrelated causes". All causes relate to the trauma. Never forget this. Trauma oftentimes is the key that unlocks the door to your systemic demise. Protect yourself.

One thing Whidden found in our example was that many things he had been exposed to "grew up" during his period without a proper immune function. No matter how healthy you think you are, there are sickness issues and "sickness seeds" within your system waiting for an opportunity to blossom. If you do not accept or understand this consider all the inoculations for sickness and disease you have undergone. All of these inoculations are "sickness seeds" sown into your system so that your system begins to build and maintain a system of anti-bodies to fight that pathogen. Over the course of a lifetime your system has many things it must fight. These inoculations may just add to the list. If you should ever have your immune system compromised by way of a shock event then all these pathogens could be released to grow unchecked and you could experience everything you were trying to avoid. Can you see this? Well, let's take it a step further as far as inoculations go...... Your system may have finite or limited resources to fight pathogens. The "sickness seeds" and other things you are exposed to can serve to overload a possibly over taxed, under equipped system for fighting, thus driving you to a deep level of sickness early.

Many conditions develop by way of our modern environment which serve to compromise the immune system. Our failure to reconcile our system with our modern environment is at the root of many of our problems. Many of our population manifest presence or overload of toxins as "allergies", reactions or as other immune deficient issues emerge. You needn't live with these problems. As we will soon see allergies are often a sign of an immune system becoming overloaded. Once we remove the "overload" situation, a great many allergies will disappear.

The modern diet and cultural issues have the body poorly prepared to manage and survive a health situation I refer to as "The Western Condition". In "The Chemical Conspiracy" book we will present a host of food issues and common practices leading to the general demise of the human body.

The Western Condition will be more fully explained, diagnosed, and scientifically explored in an accompanying volume to this book set. To brief you, the "Western Condition" is a general, over-arching situation or condition of the human body to include virtually all modern sicknesses. Basically all common sicknesses of this generation including cancer require a common set of denominators or factors to exist. These common factors bring us to what we call "The Western Condition" which is in essence an umbrella term to cover all known sickness of the Western developed world. We will develop this idea further as we go. Meanwhile, if we were to grow a garden we would prepare the soil for the crops we wished to plant. In the same light, our modern changes to the environment have materially altered the "soil" of the human body making it rich and fertile ground for sickness. Once we recognize what is causing this general decline in health we can demonstrate a reconciliation approach as we do within these books to bring back wellness and destroy sickness.

The key is to understand that virtually everyone has altered "soil" of the body/environment and the alteration will consume the health resources of virtually everyone you know sooner or later. It is far simpler and easier to kill cancer and all its associated issues than to explain it. The conventional approach has not, and will not work, so let's abandon convention and look at how simple it is to create health............We study how to eradicate the Western Condition. By changing the condition conducive to creating death we increase life. Point is that is not nearly as important to put things "in" the body to create this change as it is to focus on what to take "out" of the body. Removal of toxins is critical. There is a natural approach that will far outpace all others.

You must realize that conventional modern medicine does not come from a study of "health". It is actually a study of "sickness". The average medical professional may be quite sick themselves, and at times appear to have a very poor understanding of health. Notice that pharmaceutical companies are massive, powerful entities who pour big money into medical schools and programs to brainwash medical professionals. In part, this financial incentive could serve to cloud the judgment of health practitioners.

In studying sickness conventional western medicine works to avert disaster, but if they changed to studying health and excellence the sickness would likely fall by the wayside because it cannot survive in a healthy body. Is that so hard to see? If not consider a concept like "chemo-therapy" for addressing cancer. When doctors prescribe "chemo" do you think they calculate how much poison it takes to kill the cancer? NO, not at all. They actually try to discern how much poison they can serve to kill the host, and then back it off just a little. They study how much poison the body (host) can take yet still recover. The theory is that the cancer is weaker than the host. If you take the host (body) just short of death often, then you test the amazing ability the human body has to recover, then eventually the host will win out over the cancer. Think about it!! They don't consider what it takes to kill the cancer. They study what it would take to KILL the HOST, and hope to aim just shy of that. Can you see how backwards this approach is? Why not go the other route? Why not make the body so healthy that the invading host is destroyed like evicting a bad tenant? I assure you the body can be made strong enough to evict foreign invaders, and this is a far better, more efficient means of fighting all sickness. It is the original plan. This is not an "alternative". This is an age old plan that has and will always work.

Once you recognize fibromyalgia, gluten reactions, high blood pressure, arthritis, cancer, AIDS/HIV, and so many other conditions are under the influence of "The Western Condition" you simply change the condition, and sickness will often flee. The difficulty for most people is this is too simple and too cheap to understand. As a culture we have been indoctrinated to think powerful things must be complicated or expensive, when in truth the opposite is true. In this so-called society we have been indoctrinated to think that people educated by special interest groups and represented by lobbying organizations have all the answers, when quite the opposite is true. If a group has a great product or process they shouldn't need lobbyists, UNLESS the people are too foolish to see the simple good.

As we proceed I will introduce a simple plan that will eliminate a host of environmental issues leading to sickness and disease. In an accompanying text ("The Chemical Conspiracy") I will give precise examples of product misuse, common oldwives tales proliferated by practitioners, and a host of very sophisticated illnesses than can be tempered or controlled using a simple process. The simple process is being kept from you by others, because it works. You will quickly be able to spot things in your environment that are negatively affecting you, and your product usage should change dramatically if you want to shift your health. Following onwards one would hope that a radical shift in social standards for products will take place, and a large movement commence with demands for specific labeling and quality of products introduced to the public.

In the accompanying text ("The Chemical Conspiracy") to follow we introduce specific conditions mis-diagnosed and mistreated by medical professionals and by our culture via old wives' tales. We show you how trauma is missed, mis-handled, and give specific treatment to address and remove localized and generalized traumas, inflammation, toxic issues, and a host of problems becoming common place in our society due to the degradation called "The Western Condition". Modern society, toxic products, and environmental influences being introduced by "modernization" are inducing cancers and virtually every sickness known to man. Advocacy groups are missing the mark because the treatment and handling is too simple for many to make money off of it. There are people enslaving others in pain for their own profiteering and gain. Get free. Read on.

CHAPTER Three
The First Key to Health Recovery: Oxygen

A problem that our test subject Whidden found was that following his accident he suffered from hyper cortisol. Cortisol is the "fight or flight" hormone. Sometimes it is called the "stress" hormone, and many with the "Western Condition" due to stress become affected by cortisol. Hyper cortisol interrupted Whidden's immune function, reallocated minerals within the body, and a cascade effect of problems occurred intermixed with a nervous disorder, respiratory acidosis, and severe brain damage.

The general demise of Whidden's condition was complicated in many ways by the ongoing stress (cortisol) while combatting injuries. The stress issues manufactured in part by litigation from the accident worked against his self-funded efforts to recover. Low immunity helped spin things out of control.

The resulting oxygen deprivation, seizures and host of maladies affecting Whidden lead to a general destruction of his health, financial, mental and emotional control. In fact, 18 months after the wreck Whidden's neurocognitive brain function was at the bottom 6% in a normal population study, he could barely walk, talk, was having severe seizures/convulsion, and was dangerously close to sleeping himself into a coma. Whidden suffered from severe high blood pressure. Under sleep studies some 3 years after the accident it was determined that his heart rate would exceed 180 beats per minute WHILE SLEEPING (!!!) leading to seizure. Whidden had ongoing signs of sepsis infection, but his immune system remained unreactive to the problem(s). There was indications of food reactions/allergies. People with his condition generally live a short life in pain, and then go into a coma in their sleep, never to awaken. The "trauma" overloads their body and they die of "unrelated causes". The body works as a machine of many parts. The effect on one part cascades to the other. In essence "chaos theory" rolls through the body when any one thing is altered out of the norm. The cascade effect or general deterioration of the body following a traumatic event is the remnant of the traumatic event. There is no such thing as an unrelated cause. We introduce the first real approach to managing the "chaos theory" of the body.

Meanwhile, Whidden was operating without any significant insurance of any form. The trucking company responsible for the rear end collision had used dubious means and more than eight crooked lawyers to avoid their liability in the accident. Whidden's own "uninsured motorist" coverage (USAA Automobile Insurance) on his vehicle refused to pay for the loss and losses related to the accident. Basically as it turns out, in some accidents the loss is so severe that if the financially responsible party delays payment long enough the victim will die and the insurance may not have to pay. For this and possibly other reasons it must have appeared beneficial to all financial interests not to pay, thus pushing Whidden into a desperate life threatening period of existence. I make this digression to the financial aspects of Whidden's accident, because in a world driven by financial and legal influences it is commonly believed that these are the routes to health and recovery. Crooked financial interests are often not looking for a health approach. They are looking for a financial mechanism to derive income. The patient/victim is thus a victim of a poorly equipped, improperly motivated system. Whidden's unique situation required that he fund, manage, direct, and develop his own recovery out of necessity, or succumb to coma and death............ (Whidden survived, reversed his situation, and remains to this day using the techniques.) This book series is in essence a series of "Survival" texts and techniques to prevent the terminally ill or terminally medicated from suffering at the hands of an ill-equipped, poorly motivated system.

Conventional medical approaches and countless medical professions failed to adequately engage Whidden's problem in large part because the appearance of lack of resources (no applicable insurance). As one can imagine the practice of medicine is a profession in which many intend to get paid. This often prevents folks from getting proper medical attention. Even those who do have some form of policy of insurance often get compromised care, because their care at times can be governed as much by the plan the medical provider has for compensation as the condition itself. Corrupt? I should think so. Understand "insurance" is not the answer. In Whidden's case the misinformation provided by the insurance carrier advising doctors coverage was expired led to doctors truncating care it seems. The insurance company in the driver seat for your health care is very dangerous. In many ways insurance coverage for healthcare guarantees you will NOT get proper care. The insurance protocols for the doctor to get paid are set for the doctor to get paid, not for the doctor to get results. Doctors do wasteful tests and prolong the patient agony at times awaiting tests so they can follow insurance protocols. Health insurance is a terrible way to insure good health.

Meanwhile, if the insurance industry really wanted to save their money they would endorse, implement and support a requirement to follow a simple health reconciliation approach that should provide overwhelmingly effective to the majority of persons, and may only cost about $50. The conventional industry's failure to develop and implement a "health" approach to purify the systems of the body seems suspect. The approach Whidden developed can boost health recovery from operations, trauma, head injury/concussions, and countless other issues. The same approach can/could/should be implemented in emergency rooms and every division of hospitals because of the universal application possible. Some of those applications and ideas are included within this book. We thank Whidden for allowing his journey to be chronicled in part in this book for the use of others.

Whidden's physical system went into near catastrophic failure multiple times. Eighteen months or so after the accident he had liquidated most of his movable assets from his hobby farm (so to speak). Nearing a veritable bankrupt situation made some survival maneuvers including refinance of some real estate to raise some cash, and then max cash advance on sets of credit cards to prepare to finance the end of life. All hope was lost.

In a last ditch effort Whidden was directed to a clinic where they had tested him 12 or so months earlier for traumatic brain injury and PTSD (Post Traumatic Stress Disorder) issues. Earlier Whidden had tested and was found to need treatment but was unable to access the system for financial and other reasons. This time Whidden tested worse than before and his condition was steadily deteriorating. Since Whidden was paying out of pocket it was at his discretion what they did and how they did it. Using a somewhat modified protocol for HBOT (Hyperbaric Oxygen Therapy) Whidden averted a potentially oncoming coma and death it seems. Whidden's initial brain cognitive function was at the bottom 6% of a statistical population group. At the end of 20 treatments he tested at about 25% level in the same group. Treatment, improvements, and testing continued and after some 60 or so treatments he was testing at 55%!!! In a brain function study he had started at near brain dead (relatively) and passed nearly half of a conventional statistical population! SHAZAM!! Healed!!! No, not really, but greatly improved.

What the HBOT treatment demonstrated is that oxygen revives the system and brain recovery more than 18 months after severe brain injury is possible. Yet, this was not the end of the oxygen story, but the beginning.

Whidden was not satisfied at a 55% operational brain cognitive level. Meanwhile, the next phase of treatments and studies at the clinic was for autistic kids, and in order to stay in the program Whidden would have to bump one of the kids from potentially their only chance at recovery. Instead of bumping a kid from his healing, the owner of the clinic introduced Whidden to other clinics, and he began bouncing around from clinic to clinic seeking help. For the next two years all of Whidden's income and cash flows went into hyperbaric oxygen therapy, studies and exploration. The hyperbaric treatments are wonderful and very helpful, but for some reason the patient could not get lasting results. Oxygen was the key to this health issue it seemed, but oxygen retention and wellness seemed to be a problem. There are/were reasons for this to be explained another time, elsewhere. (See Whidden's book on Hyperbaric Oxygen Therapy, HBOT or contact him through his newly opened "retreat".).

Through this study one overarching concept became abundantly clear. A key to health is revealed. An oxygen shortage, deficit or deprivation is a key to sickness, in fact for the purposes of this book and the majority of health issues we can make the bold statement that some form of oxygen deprivation is the root of virtually all sickness in the body. Oxygen is a requirement for health. That seems simple enough, however what is not so clear is that localized or system loss of oxygenation to the body may in one perspective be the root cause/effect of every sickness of the "Western Condition". It is possible to see now how every sickness one can think of can most likely be eradicated with the proper use of oxygen. I will now begin to show you how and why this is true, and take you through a virtually universal approach to health that in practical application will likely harm no one, and will likely help everyone. It is very effective, extremely cheap, and very simple, with universal application. It works. It will work for you and everyone you know for virtually any and every condition. It can and should be used before any and all other approaches, and in conjunction with any and all approaches, and can be used subsequent to any and all approaches. The main problem with this approach is that it is so universally successful and simple that it should reduce doctor visits and all medical dependencies by up to 80%, and your health providers do not want you to know about that. It may cost them some business. Meanwhile, your insurance company, your family, and your boss want you to follow this protocol because you will live longer and stronger, you will be more productive, will miss less work, will depend less on the government and insurance, and will be a better family member. You'll be nicer to be around. Can you handle that? Do others a favor and give it a try.

What a little research will show you is that virtually every sickness known to man requires some anomaly within the system to open the door to let the sickness in. In many, if not most, situations that door opening the way for sickness is some physical blockage, a pinched nerve, or something that starves nutrient and oxygen flow to a region of the body. This initiates a cascade effect of problems. Conventional medicine today addresses the symptom, such as the headache, without determining what is causing the headache. (Headaches are often caused by oxygen deprivation, thus aspirin as a blood thinner is a key to getting more oxygen to the brain. Seems simple? Read on.)   The Western Condition is plagued in part with people seeking immediate gratification for their immediate (and at times idiotic) demands. Meanwhile, the medical practitioner knows that if they placate the patient's symptoms, the root problem remains and they will return. The pain of the patient becomes the income stream of the medical community. If that were not true, they would introduce you to this simple system and let you make your decisions.

The headache as an example was initially treated by aspirin. Meanwhile the aspirin primarily acts as a blood thinner, and it allows blood with nutrients and OXYGEN to the region of the brain. This works much of the time, however it is a temporary fix. Since people do not look for long term relief but only short term, the patient will keep coming back, or use (misuse) an approach because the approach failed to address the long term oxygen deprivation issues.

Oxygen brings life, and understanding the oxygen environ-ment and what the body needs to manage oxygen is a major component of health. I will not explain all this science in this version, but rather give you a process to follow to wellness and explain the science in another volume.

CHAPTER Four
The story of the "Three henchmen"

Left unattended oxygen deficits open the door for our first set of predators. I refer to the predators as the Three Henchmen. The "Three Henchmen" are the three simple components that do almost all the dirty work of sickness.

The "Three Henchmen" are what brings about the effect of much sickness. They are simply listed as: bacteria, fungus, and protozoa.

When Whidden lost his immune system he started breaking things down into categories. Conventional medical systems get caught trying to narrow things down, when, if they broadened their approach more success in treatment could occur. The Three Henchmen (bacteria, fungus, and protozoa) do the damage, causing the pain and suffering of almost all conditions. Without them, then there may be no pain, no suffering, and no existence or evidence of sickness; thus you would be healthy.

The first thing to understand as we generalize about the Three Henchmen is there are generally two types. There are aerobic (needs oxygen) and anaerobic (dies in the presence of oxygen) versions of the bacteria, fungus, and protozoa. As you can see, generalizing has uncovered the fact that one type/style of the Three Henchmen can be killed by oxygen/oxygenation alone. The largest group of toxic flora in the body is anaerobic and thus intolerant to oxygen. Isn't this amazing!!?? Potentially half or more of all sickness problems are caused by either bacteria, fungus, or protozoa which are anaerobic! All we have to do is find a way to super oxygenate the system and many pathogens in the system die instantly. Amazingly simple!

This concept will remain critical throughout establishing our groundwork and proofs for this approach.

As you will soon see, CO_2 is a byproduct of all cellular activity, and when it accumulates, it acts to block the path of oxygen. All we must do is work towards removing CO_2, and oxygen fills the space and potentially half of all health problems disappear. Can you see how easy it is? Read this again. I will repeat and re-use this approach numerous times in this book. Begin to get your head around the root of your problem.

To repeat, by definition the three types of organisms that cause much pain and suffering in the body are anaerobic in nature and admission of oxygen, by way of oxygenation techniques, will kill it. No need for drugs, antibiotics, or pharmaceuticals. CO_2 and oxygen cannot co-exist, so the presence of CO_2 often blocks the existence of oxygen. A very simple CO_2 removal program will flood the body with oxygen, and thus kill many pathogens. The flooding with oxygen feeds the body with nutrition and healing begins. A radical transformation of even bad situations can take place.

A large percentage (potentially 80%?) of the "Three Henchmen" will die in the presence of oxygen, and presence of the "Three Henchmen" in turn tells us there is an oxygenation problem.

We will show you how to kill them very simply in our Acidic Gas Reconciliation approach. Eureka! Many of you will start healing before you finish this book! Most of you who understand and apply the concepts will walk in wellness for a long(er) period of time. People with terminal issues will increase life quality, duration, and eradicate most pain without any harmful drugs or side effects.

(Note: A poorly discussed, poorly addressed epidemic of parasitic infections will be addressed in our "Digestive Disorder" book. Limited time and space prevents it here.)

CHAPTER Five

Fungus

(Before starting this chapter, get a bucket of hot water. Throw 2-3 handfuls of baking soda in the bucket and begin soaking your feet in such solution as you work through the rest of the book.)

Following onwards from the general study of the Three Henchmen we need to focus on one in particular, the FUNGUS. We must move quickly. I will make several bold statements which you can confirm through your own study later.

The acidic/neutral body of those in the Western Culture makes humans a seed bed for fungus. If fungus is not treated it will work to destroy the host. Accurate study of the action and life cycle of fungus will show us it does three things in the body: 1) Robs resources we need 2) Blocks resources we need 3) Releases neurotoxins in the system.

Fungus clearly takes resources from the body which we need to survive. This seems clear. In so doing it robs resources.............. Meanwhile there are components in the body that are absorbed or utilized in the human body in tandem with something else. If the component used in tandem is consumed by the fungus, then the other associated component is effectively blocked from full utilization in the body, and thus a spiraling down effect of the human body is begun.

The lifecycle of virtually all cellular life in the universe produces some kind of waste or byproduct. The byproducts of fungus are waste to the fungus, but to the human body this is a very dangerous neurotoxin. Neurotoxins from fungus plow the ground necessary for cancer(s) and a host of other problems. Blocking fungus should be an early effort and approach to virtually every sickness in the Western society, because fungus is often a sign of drastic deterioration underway in the body systems.

Fungal neurotoxins create the pain of arthritis and virtually all joint pain. Fungus must die.

Virtually all common fungus in the universe requires a near neutral pH environment. Since our body is supposed to be slightly alkaline at 7.4 pH then we are dangerously close at all times to a neutral environment (pH of 7.0). For this reason we should make efforts to avoid many acidic products in/near our body. Otherwise we risk inviting fungus outgrowth in our system.

In virtually all attempts at fighting infection the conventional approach is to shift the environment locally or generally in the host outside that area tolerable for the infectious issue. At times an acidic approach to remove fungus (bacteria/protozoa) may work over the very short haul, but will virtually always lead to a recurring event and additional sickness. Clearly and simply, products that are relatively acidic to the body remove/destroy minerals. This is generally very bad. Our processed foods and drinks are often lacking proper minerals. Our products by way of poor design and understanding are acidic. Thus very poorly implemented science creates a seedbed for fungus in the body, thus general deterioration of the body, known as The Western Condition. Fungus is a sign of your lack of health and must be addressed. It is so severe I would recommend that you treat it irrespective of whether or not you see it or know it is there. Often people are in denial, so just treat for the stuff, and get it behind you.

(Note: An acidic approach to fungus would potentially wipe out the fungus initially, but your system must pass back through the neutral stage on its way to normalizing at 7.4 pH, so an acidic approach is unwise.)

Fungus seems to have little use within the body other than decomposition when the body is dead. In my opinion the presence of fungus is the process of decomposition and death/dying, thus life may require you remove/exterminate all fungus. Fungus will compromise many, most, if not all, approaches to health, so focus on its removal for a time. This approach may anger some, but when you are sick and you see presence of fungus this should tell you two things: 1) Your body and the area of the fungus is too close to acidic/neutral 2) you have the presence of neurotoxins.

Interestingly, fungus often shows an exterior sign on the body. If you approach your practitioner correctly and ask them if the external fungal sign is really the sign of an internal fungal problem, invariably all the honest ones will say, "Yes". Treating an external fungal growth without treating its internal component may be a waste of time. I advocate all people in the western culture to immediately and persistently pursue methods to kill fungus. In our process we will show a couple of simple methods to begin to address fungus. (More radical methods may be needed to get a handle on fungus. I would consider this urgent for many people. Remember, fungus opens the door for many sicknesses and cancer.)

In the study of agriculture one sees that in order to grow a certain plant one must "prepare the soil" for the desired plant/product. The body works the same way. Just as one adds or removes minerals from soil to prepare land for growing plants, we as a culture "prepare the soil of our bodies" by creating acidic or alkaline environments. The person who allows acidic gas to buildup in their body becomes acidic, and thus a target for fungus, cancer and virtually every known sickness to mankind (The Western Condition). The person/community that allows a healthy alkaline body to approach acidic conditions is asking for problems.

In our studies of cancer we have found that every person we have checked with who has cancer also has fungus. It is almost like cancer is a form of fungus, or an outgrowth of fungus. In studying it superficially it seems to me to be almost a "chicken and egg" situation as to which came first the fungus or the cancer. The assumption I am working under is that the fungus while consuming and blocking resources and releasing neurotoxins is what allows the environment for cancer to begin. It is almost like it is the farm tool that prepares the soil (body) for the growth of cancer. If this assumption is true, then it would seem that one can eradicate the fungus, and then destroy the possibility of cancer forming...............Also, if one already has cancer, then the fungal action of robbing, blocking resources, and releasing neurotoxins in conjunction with a cancer is doing the same thing is just too much of a toll on the body. In either event before or after cancer the fungus must be killed. Killing fungus is the first step to removing cancer. Kill all fungus and keep killing it. Time will prove us correct, that cancer is greatly diminished.

The problems associated with fungus are so clear one must wonder why more people are not talking about it. A simple, repetitive means needs to be set and if fungus is wiped out or reconciled in the body on a regular basis, then one's health would have far fewer problems to deal with. Killing fungus cannot be overstressed. The medical profession has ignored the internal effects of fungus too long.

(I am not one often to advocate products, but there are products on the market that are said to block enzymes needed for the maintenance of cell walls of fungus. It would seem that blocking an enzyme needed for cell wall maintenance is a good thing. It is like pulling the rug out from under their existence.

Many would find this and other such approaches very worthwhile. There are herbal approaches as well that have an effect.)

I would urge anyone/everyone to go to whatever source you use (medical/pharmaceutical/health food store/etc.) and start fighting fungus. Fight it as if it is there, whether you see it or not. Fungus may be at the root of much (all?) evil in the body. Fight it and keep fighting it. There are a number of reasons why it will outlive the basic medical approach to killing it. I will explain as we go. Kill Fungus, keep killing fungus.

One thing to understand as we move to the next step is that FUNGUS LOVES IRON! Iron accumulation leads to fungus accumulation. Fungus accumulation should tell us there is an iron accumulation............

As it appears, fungus is in existence in all cancer, and the neurotoxins and environment form the path for cancer; then foundationally removing fungus is the first step in ridding the body of cancer. In so doing, it is also the main line of prevention of cancers. As we see that fungus is integrally connected to IRON in the environment, we should explore iron and its effects on the pathogenic relationship of iron, fungus, and cancer.

Fungus Facts:

1) The body does not need fungus.

2) Virtually all fungus in the universe exists at about neutral pH (7.0).

3) The human body is designed to function at about 7.4 pH so any existence/propagation of fungus in or on the body is a sign of sickness by way of low pH.

4) Presence of fungus indicates an acidosis condition in the body (Low pH).

5) Presence of fungus indicates low oxygenation often by way of low mineralization.

6) External signs of fungus indicate an internal fungus problem.

7) Fungus
   a)   Robs resources your need.
   b)   Blocks resources you need.
   c)   Releases neurotoxins you do not need.

8) Fungus accompanies all cancers.

9) Fungus often "feeds" on iron accumulations. Iron is required by most fungus, and the iron issue will become very important as we read on.

10) The environment needed for fungus is the same as needed for cancer. Killing the first one (fungus) will often help rid the body of cancer. The shift of the environment to remove or eradicate fungus will often prove to be the shift to eradicate the cancer.

11) To this point in history medical practitioners have failed to alert and educate the public at large to the seriousness of fungus and the above points.

12) Fungus is reaching epidemic proportions with virtually all small children in the Western society having forms of fungus. Children with fungus are often not treated because the conventional "medical" approach uses very harsh drugs that may not be necessary. If they merely focused on the pH shift of the host then fungus could be tempered.

13) Fungus is likely the "gateway" sickness to cancer and a host of other issues.

14) Poor nutrition and environmental influences allow fungus to be common. I would estimate that more than one half of the population has untreated, ongoing fungal issues that are allowed to proliferate in part because of the failure to understand the serious internal nature of fungal infections, and in part because of failure of the medical/health industry to properly educate and address this concern. (Meanwhile, allowing fungus to remain relatively obscure will allow a host of cancers and other sicknesses to develop, morph, and attack the body. Ignoring fungus is "good" for the cancer business, because it is at the root of all that is evil in that business.)

15) Meanwhile, a shift in body chemistry by removing acidosis conditions should serve to temper and/or eradicate fungal growth. Shifting the body pH to a higher alkaline level is likely the core focus of every "raw", vegan, or "health food" diet". Meanwhile, there may be an easier, faster way to shift the ills of the body than by diet. The alkaline emersion approach would significantly and instantaneously shift a sick body to a more healthy body. Read on.

CHAPTER Six

MRI: *The Cause and Cure of Cancer*

(Soak feet in baking soda water solution. Do you see bubbles? If you get the mix right you will see bubbles. There must be bubbles....)

If you can understand or control the feeding mechanism of virtually anything, then you can control that thing. Understanding how cancer and other sickness "feeds" itself is critical for eradication or extermination of the problem. Many people know that MRI's are used for detecting anomalies in the body. Meanwhile what is an MRI and what does it do? I will keep it simple and state that MRI stands for "Magnetic Resonance Imaging".

The name MRI (Magnetic Resonance Imaging) begs the question, "What influences magnetic issues in the body and what metal in the universe affects or is most affected by magnetism?" Iron. Iron is the most influenced metal by magnetism. There is an overwhelming possibility that a "cluster" of iron would affect magnetic fields within a region of the body during an MRI.

Seeking iron clusters (magnetic anomalies) leads us to the simple question as to what part of the body supports or uses iron, and the simple answer is hemoglobin the main oxygen component of blood. Surely practitioners and theorists knew this and didn't need me to tell you this. With this knowledge we can simply deduce how cancer feeds itself. Once you know how to feed cancer, then we will know how to starve it and we begin another approach to disarming the cancer. Can you see how simple and intuitive it is? It is really no more complicated than this.

Some MRI's today have an accompanying injection to help illuminate certain issues. The injection before an MRI to enhance the image only circulates where you have circulation, and thus accentuates the iron clusters, glucose uptakes, and/or anomalies with low circulation. The results are reasonably the same, they are seeking iron clusters and functional irregularities.

Iron accumulation and related anomalies within the body are most typically the result of blood or circulation irregularities. Iron deficiencies are associated with oxygen deficits because of low hemoglobin which typically carries oxygen in the blood.

A surplus of iron gives rise to a number of issues within the body, and often cancer uses excess iron as the feeding mechanism to support it. Read that again, cancer which shows up on an MRI is manipulating iron for a FEEDING SYSTEM for the cancer. If you study/understand how the cancer is fed, then you can control feeding and effectively starve the cancer. A system to initiate the starvation of the cancer will be explained within this book. It is extremely safe and can be conducted by virtually anyone, anytime, as often as you wish without regulation.

Iron and iron accumulations/utilization is a requirement of many disease-based pathogens. Fungus thrives in an iron rich, low oxygen environment. An abundance or excess of iron commonly affects liver, heart and endocrine glands. Clinical issues associated with high levels of iron are cirrhosis of the liver, diabetes, arthritis, testicular failure, grey skin discoloration, joint and bone pain, to name a few. Our approach will help rectify many of these conditions while shifting environment to one in which cancer cannot survive. This is why we call it the "Western Condition". Virtually all known sickness stems from the same set of conditions. By thwarting the

"Western Condition" we have a veritable "silver bullet" to treat or pre-treat or prevent all common sickness and disease.

Again, iron provision and/or accumulation is required for some pathogens, all fungus, and cancer itself to use as a tool. They will all coexist especially the anaerobic issues, and if you can reconcile the environment properly of the right component in the right way, they will all disappear. Dissipating the iron build-up would control and begin to kill the pathogens harbored in the body.

The body is loaded with iron which is good for the host/body; however stagnation of flow, absence of oxygen, presence of relatively acidic solution, while iron is present opens the door for a host of sickness, fungus, and infectious issues. The fungus and cancer itself, in coordination with a host of other pathogens hammer away on the foothold they establish in the body. The key in part is to address the pathogens working in cooperation with the cancer to increase the body's immune reaction and preserve resources.

Returning to a general discussion on cancer will help understand the problem. Cancer is simply stated as a rogue pathogen cell cluster existing within the body. The cell cluster (cancer) must provide two things that all living organisms must have to survive. It must have a way to feed and a way to excrete toxins. All we must do is better understand these two systems, disable one or both as described within this book and those to come, and we win the battle of cancer. It is really that simple.

Some believe that cancerous cells are everywhere and they coexist looking for an opportunity to reside. I don't buy into this necessarily, but it is expedient to accept that to make a point. It is reasonably simple to see that cancer cells are opportunistic, and the concept of chemo therapy itself is based on the concept that they are weak cells or at least weaker than the body. (FYI: Conventional chemotherapy focuses on taking the body to the brink of destruction, and the stronger cells (the body) will survive.) My approach is diametrically opposed to chemotherapy in that we strengthen the body so that it overcomes the cancer. In our approach, quality and length of life is improved with treatment with no troublesome side-effects.

The opportunist cancer cells seem to follow fungal outgrowths in the body. Fungus in many ways helps prepare the way for cancer to exist and facilitates the spreading. Treating the fungus helps treat the cancer. It frees up resources and boosts immune, while dismantling the environment cancer needs to grow.

Fungus requires a low oxygen, low flow region to exist and thrive. Fungus does three things: 1) consumes resources you need, 2) blocks resources you need, 3) releases neurotoxins which damage tissue.

The three effects of fungus open the doorway and prepare the soil of the body to propagate cancer. The acidic nature of the neurotoxins consumes minerals and alkaline based resources thus lowering oxygenation. The harder "metals" within the body are the last consumed, thus a build-up of iron commences in the toxic gas/fluid bed of the fungus. An acidic electrolytic solution with a heavy metal like iron in it forms an electric "charge" just like a "lead-acid" battery used in your car. The electrical charge with iron creates a "magnetic anomaly" within your body. MRI which measures "Magnetic Resonance Imaging" photographs magnetic anomalies. THINK PEOPLE!! Utilization of MRI demonstrated the ability to understand and cure the sickness.

Iron accumulation in the body in an electrolytic (acid) solution (localized acidosis) creates MAGNETISM!! Magnetism attracts IRON, and thus the cancer is using magnetism to "feed" itself. Once this is understood then manipulating the electronic and/or magnetic field around the anomaly/body can disarm the cancer and starve its feeding mechanism. I will describe several means to do this, but give one simple, straight forward approach that anyone/everyone can employ at low cost, without medical or government intervention. Cancer must flee.

The iron accumulation arises in a puddle of slightly acidic body solution (localized acidosis), that consumes all alkaline and oxygen/nutrition management resources. The accumulation of iron as a residue becomes electrically and thus magnetically charged. It continues to draw in and consume resources, thus the feeding has begun. The accumulation of bio-waste creates an ever increasing storehouse of iron, thus magnetism (feeding) increases. By merely dissipating the iron, and/or reducing acidity, and/or increasing oxygenation/circulation the growth can be stifled and the body reconciled. (Starve cancer by reducing localized acidosis and dissipating iron build-up.)

Death from cancer often stems from a localized acidosis condition that becomes a more generalized acidosis condition, thus lowering oxygen utilization in the body. The lack of mineralization associated with fungal outgrowths, cancers, and acidosis often strike the kidneys and people often die from the kidney failure, not from the cancer itself. Preserving the kidneys, thwarts generalized acidosis. Striving to overcome acidosis assists in overcoming localized acidosis while preserving the kidneys. Overcoming localized acidosis stimulates total body circulation, and the cancer starts to starve.

Unfortunately, (or fortunately?) we hear stories of MRI or various forms of imaging that shows cancer and through some twist of events the cancer or mass miraculously "disappears". Under test I have demonstrated that the error is most likely (and usually) in the original diagnostic imaging and reading of the results. A localized acidosis condition to most practitioners appears as a mass, and 40-50 years into the technology they are not aware of this, nor are they advising their patients...............Following onwards from the errors of implementation of diagnostics we will find that very often (almost always?) the image they look at using conventional modern technology is a toxic gas buildup. Reconciliation of toxic gases in the body is not only a suitable way to improve imaging, but it is likely the only real treatment to cure process.

Reconciliation of Toxic Gases in the body will likely eradicate all possibility for cancer and most other sicknesses.

Shortly in the treatment recommendation we will show you how to reverse the electrolytic power struggle for the cells in your body, boost body performance, increase circulation and thus oxygenation, and dissipate the neurotoxins which clears the way for cancer growth. In the process we will strengthen the organs that typically fail, leading to cancer death. In so doing your body will see a performance boost, and will recognize the pathogen we call cancer and attack/reject the cancer as if it was an invader similar to the way the body rejects a splinter of wood under the skin. Given time it protects itself and ejects the splinter. In fighting cancers it will reduce the cancer by way of starvation and begin moving it to the surface with it dissipating at or before arrival at the surface.

In this and future writings we will explain how and why this works. For now, simply follow the enclosed procedure which should work to avoid or to treat cancers and most other sickness within the body. What we find in the "Western Condition" is that mankind has altered the environment of the body faster than the body has been able to adapt or reconcile. Mankind, environment, and science itself have created and sustained a host of sickness issues for profit. By shifting the body condition, almost all known sicknesses (cancer included), will die and/or leave the body. It is too simple to miss. The only ones this will not work for is those who fail to follow instructions, or attempt to modify the approach.

Once you use magnetic resonance to detect a problem (MRI), you acknowledge that magnetic and metallic issues are at the root of the problem. Changing the chemistry of the body as it relates to those core issues will likely resolve any issue detectable by the science. Can you see this? Meanwhile, you needn't understand how MRI functions, to understand how to overcome what it finds. An eighth grader can understand, research and employ the treatment while seeking a cure.

As we move along I introduce you to a simple concept called "Bubble Diagnostics". It is a simple, cheap, effective and natural means of BOTH diagnosis and therapy. This method uses a simple solution emersion concept to detect localized areas of damage and sickness. The body will literally "bubble" in a "simple solution" from where the problem emanates. It is simple really. Instead of just detecting a problem like an expensive MRI or whatever would do, it effectively relieves issues while showing you where the issue is located. The emersion solution as recommended (Simple Solution hence the name of the book) will not only relieve inflammation, pain, swelling, while killing anaerobic bacteria your body will "bubble" as the site or location of the problems. This is both effective therapeutically and diagnostically. By reducing inflammation and toxic gases in the body it will enhance and improve other approaches. It will immediately begin a reconciliation process of the body missing in our modern culture.

MRI Facts:

1) MRI means "magnetic resonance imaging".
2) Mineral irregularities (iron/manganese) form and flow irregularities likely create the primarily "magnetic anomalies" imaged by MRI.
3) Iron/Manganese irregularities indicate circulation and oxygenation irregularities.
4) Iron "build-up" in an acid rich environment will show up

on an MRI because of the combined interaction of components (iron, acid, fungus, etc.)

5) Availability of "MRI" as a tool to image the body may give rise to fungal concerns, because certain magnetic anomalies images by MRI require ideal fungal conditions for imaging to work. Shifting the body environment would eradicate the anomaly, and thus often the problem causing the sickness.

6) Any attempt or use of MRI to image the body should signal to the person that they could/should be considering Alkaline Emersion (Acid Gas Reconciliation) as outlined herein.

7) The theory and technology required to envision, understand, design, build, and operate MRI equipment is definitely more complicated than simply understanding and correcting the anomaly within the body. (This should upset people!)

8) Iron build-up in the body is often associated with a localized acidosis condition. Acidosis in the body manifests itself by way of acidic gas and acidic fluids (that produce acidic gas) in the body.

CHAPTER Seven

The Key to Sickness, CO2

(Use baking soda liberally. Soak your feet in baking soda water and you'll see CO_2 leaving the body while you read about it.)

This chapter should be a part of all classes on Health 101. It is upsetting how simple this is, yet no one seems to discuss it.

CO_2, otherwise known as Carbon Dioxide is a gaseous by-product of cells in the body. All cells in the body (healthy and unhealthy) must deal with their own CO_2 issues and the CO_2 issues of other cells and components of the body. CO_2 by design is present in all healthy tissues. Meanwhile, CO_2 in abundance or stagnation is present in virtually all sickness. Read that again!! CO_2 accumulation is associated with virtually ALL known sicknesses, illnesses, and "conditions" of concern. There is no better place in the world to start a healing process than management and removal of excess CO_2.

CO_2 accumulation has and will always be at the core of all sickness. It has never been different, and it never will be. How in the world did "we" miss this? Why hasn't anyone told us? Think how simple and intuitive this is. Why haven't any of these "research institutes" or health organizations shared this simple, undeniable FACT? Since CO_2 is by definition accumulated in virtually every unhealthy cell, then the management and removal is critical to any short term or long term health approach. In my opinion there is no better, faster, cheaper, or more effective approach to wellness than to focus on removal of excess CO_2. We will show you how to address this, and most will find themselves to be pain free in 10 minutes or less, with a general state of health improved. Everyone thus far tested shows amazing signs of success. (The only ones seeing no or low success seem to not follow instructions.)

The simple way to remove low amounts of CO_2 generally throughout the body is to hyperventilate. Meanwhile notice any dog you have ever seen. Have you ever noticed a dog "hassle" or breath heavily with their tongue hanging out? They will do this "more" if in captivity or in a house. This is what the dog uses to rid his system of short term CO_2 increases. They know it; we have lost the simple knowledge and sense to remove sickness. The dog knows. You do not. Hyperventilation will have limited success for humans, but there are other easy ways.

(Note: I would encourage people with headaches and such to try heavy breathing or hyperventilation intermittently to see how it works. In your hyperventilation experiments, practice breathing IN deeper and deeper and deeper. Don't hold your breath just breath IN deeper each time. Make this a conscious effort throughout your day. You will begin to see improvements. It will work to rid many headaches once you understand how to do it properly. In cases where it does not work, it is likely because you did it wrong. Almost all headaches are a sign of oxygen deficits and CO_2 excess, so it should work.)

We are seeing people rid themselves of migraines and/or headaches short term using hyperventilation. This uncovers a need for oxygen in the brain, and any other approach to headaches that does not increase oxygenation may be foolhardy. Oxygenation by some means must occur or the brain begins dying. (Our next book on Head Injuries/Concussions will address migraines/headaches directly and give a more palatable approach, cause, and cure for headaches of all kind. Stay tuned!)

When a person takes an aspirin for a headaches they merely thin the blood allowing more oxygenated blood to enter the brain area. Oxygenation is the key. Oxygenation by definition removes CO_2. Animals know about this and attempt to manage theirs. Mankind has a CO_2 sensor at the base of their brain that in theory tells him when/how to breathe to keep the brain cavity properly oxygenated. In our "guinea pig" Mr Whidden he lost this management function through concussion. For that reason we had to explore ways to effectively remove and manage excess CO_2 because his system lost that "hassling" or breathing reaction.

Man has somehow dumbed down their senses and understanding of these simple things. Purveyors of products are keeping mankind ignorant so they can continue selling products. The failure to address the real problem and the continued misuse of products are often what are bringing about a generalized sickness condition in mankind that we call, "The Western Condition".

On occasion we are told that cramps in the body are the absence of minerals. This may or may not be true. The REAL CAUSE of cramps is the presence of CO_2. When your doctor advises you that you need minerals to deal with cramps, this is not necessarily true. Cramps and almost every dull nagging ache/pain, every headache, every seizure, every inflammation, every "condition" you have ever had was a result of too much CO_2. Remove the CO_2 and in most cases you remove the problem. It is really that simple.

Minerals in the body help and hurt you with a cramp or CO_2 issue. Firstly CO_2 is a toxic, acidic gas to the system. Minerals are "consumed" by the acid. The medical industry is often turning blind eye to the FACT that an acidic body is a sick body. An acidic body chemistry consumes soft metals/minerals that your body needs for proper electrolytic and cellular growth, so ingesting more minerals into a toxic body will likely create more toxic gas for a period. It may provide temporary relief, but it will not provide long term relief. The key is to remove the

CO2/acid while increasing mineralization. This will create a profound health shift that done correctly will reduce substantially the number of doctor visits. CO2 which is a waste gas in your body exists in excess amounts in every area of sickness you have or will ever have. Removing CO2 is more important than you can imagine, and simpler, too. Why hasn't anyone told you?

When we show you how to remove CO2 from the body many will feel it relaxing much like a visit for a massage or to a chiropractor. What these practitioners do often is manipulate tissue to release or shift CO2. By removing CO2 altogether you can get the effect of service without leaving home. By employing our methods in conjunction with their services many will find a veritable fountain of youth.

Why is this so effective? CO2 and other toxic gases in the system actually "take up space" in the body. The most critical problem is that CO2 and toxic gases takes up space where OXYGEN belongs!! Remember when we introduced the first key to health was OXYGEN!?? Well, the first key to sickness is CO2. Removal of CO2 is critical in all health situations, yet has been overlooked by the majority of health practitioners and approaches.

With CO2 in the way of oxygen in the cells, then oxygenation or the process of supplying viable oxygen to the body is blocked. CO2 accumulation in the body is most often why you perceive you have a "cramp". Flushing the CO2 out of the system will remove the cramp and its components actually and naturally. Taking minerals may help some, but will help much more once you remove the CO2. Removal of CO2 makes your mineral consumption infinitely more effective because the minerals are not consumed by the acid, and there is not as much toxic gas created in the system. Irrespective, the best initial approach is to remove CO2. By removing CO2 I can show you how to become immediately pain free. Pay attention and do as you are told, and you'll be pain free. So far, the only ones this process fails are those who fail to follow instructions.

CO_2 is often the gas that blocks oxygen in the system, thus allowing the "Three Henchmen" (bacteria, fungus, and protozoa) to exist in their anaerobic form. Once CO_2 is removed, they are exposed to O_2 and die. This is powerful to understand! (Often THE THREE HENCHMEN DIE in the presence of oxygen, thus removal of CO_2 is a HUGE benefit to your health.)

CO_2 is an insulating gas in the body. CO_2 often makes you perceive it is hotter than it really is. CO_2 and toxic gas present in your system is the reason you "perceive" you need air-conditioning. CO_2 accumulation in the system acts as an insulator in your body and makes your body hold heat. If you got rid of your excess CO_2 you would be far more heat tolerant.............. Think for a minute. Your grandparents may not have had air-conditioning, yet they got along just fine. The changing of our diets and internal environment is causing CO_2 build up in our systems that they never had to worry about. CO_2 buildup in the system is the number one component of the "Western Condition" which leads to all other conditions and degradations of the system. You are dying from excess CO_2 as are your kids, friends, and family. Every condition of sickness in the body requires excess CO_2 to exist. Removal of CO_2 solves hundreds of health problems. We will help heal 100 million people this year if each of you will share this book. Everyone needs to know, and not enough people are sharing this concept.

CO_2 removal is the most effective way to reduce a fever (if and when you think you need to do this.) Medical practitioners who fail to reduce CO_2 in the body when trying to reduce/control fever appear to be misguided.

CO_2 buildup is a direct resultant of all heat stroke patients. Failure to remove and reconcile the CO_2 levels in the body is another failure of practitioners to reconcile these conditions.

CO_2 is a "greenhouse" gas. It operates as an insulator. The problem is that if/when you hold it in your system then your system is running too hot, and YOU ARE HEATING UP THE EARTH! Let it out!! (Note: CO_2 accumulation IN the body makes one perceive it is hotter than it really is due to the insulator effect of the gas in the system. Reduction in CO_2 in the body, would allow many to change their thermostats in the summer, reduce the amount of air conditioning they use, reduce their power bills, reduce their energy consumption; and the release of CO_2 from the human body would thus have an overall positive effect on the environment. The accumulation of CO_2 in the body costs our society and environment abnormal amounts. Everyone you know has a CO_2 build up at this very moment. Check and see. It is simple to correct. Directions are within.)

Every pain, seizure, concussion, stroke, trauma situation, and mental condition since time eternal was affected in large part by presence of CO_2 in excess, thus reduction of oxygen. Reconciling the equation does not require pharmaceuticals. Simply removing the toxic gas build-up will actually create a "siphon" of sorts that will "wick" in the oxygen and nutrition you need. Nearly instant healing can happen in many circumstances with long term good effects, simply and inexpensively. Repetition of the approach is needed if you continue factors in your environment that lead you to the condition of sickness, but there is a harmless approach available for you to better sustain life. Acidic Gas Reconciliation as outlined in this book would solve most health issues it seems.

I advocate using an Alkaline Emersion (Acidic Gas Reconciliation) approach which will allow many to heal people in short order. Often they first see themselves rendered pain free in minutes. When CO_2 buildups are gone, the pain is often gone. Once people understand how to manage pain more effectively then they can at times get rid of many/most of their pain medications. Pain medications and their side effects seem to be the root of many health problems for sick people. Once the pain meds are gone, often the anti-depressants, anti-diarrheal, and a host of other medicines can be eliminated. This is a huge breakthrough for the consumer who is actually being consumed by commercial medical interests. Break free!

Do not waste your time/money on CO_2 testing at the doctor's office. You must understand that the "Western Condition" characterized by elevated CO_2 and low oxygenation is already past epidemic proportions in our population. Virtually everyone you know who lives in our society is already plagued with it. We see it in the form of high blood pressure and a host of misdiagnosed conditions leading to cancer. (See "The Chemical Conspiracy" book which shares a number of health misconceptions.) Everyone you know is on the road to death from the Western Condition, so when the medical industry determines what is considered "average" or "normal" for CO_2 levels, then NORMAL is a prescription for slow death. NORMAL in our society is actually HIGH! We as a people group have entirely too much CO_2 as a general population. We are severely unhealthy, and by default/nature even those whom you perceive to be "healthy" have high levels of CO_2 because of physical training and such.

The point is that if you are in the normal spectrum of blood CO_2 then you are just as sick as every other sick person. Being normal is very dangerous.............Pass on testing. Begin an approach for CO_2 elimination and you will see radical results.

All forms of breathing dysfunction, asthma, allergy, and conditions of COPD, cystic fibrosis, and a host of related conditions would be GREATLY improved by my simple CO_2 removal program. Removal of CO_2 from the system demands the body provide oxygen and nutrition to the tissue and the breathing issues become quickly reconciled. Life improves.

The key to sickness and health is not in testing. It is far, far easier to remove excess CO_2 than to test for it, and EVERY-ONE YOU KNOW has excess CO_2. It is a condition of the environment we live in. EVERY PERSON IN THE WEST-ERN WORLD has TOO MUCH CO_2.

Removing excess CO_2 will cost very small money. It is cheaper for most to remove excess CO_2 than the travel cost and time to get to the doctor's office. Smart people will begin to cut testing out of the loop and solve your excess CO_2 now.

The presence of CO_2 is often related in ways to the circulatory system. Often the recommendation for more exercise predominantly works as a flushing system to introduce more oxygen to the system while ridding the body of CO_2. The problem is that exercise creates more CO_2 and the cycle continues. I am not against exercise, I am just stating fact.

The body reacts to trauma by creating inflammation which stops flow. This is good initially as it may keep you from bleeding to death, however the inflammation reaction must be reversed, and not many focus on simple methods to reverse inflammation reaction........... The problem exists because as soon as flow of nutrient rich, oxygenated fluids in the body stops flowing, the oxygen is consumed or is literally "cooked out", and CO_2 is the main byproduct. The absence of oxygen and presence of CO_2 produces pain/inflammation. (Pain is that simple in most cases. Pain = presence of CO_2 and absence of Oxygen).

Most medical approaches focus on putting things into the body, thus producing a "log-jam" in the system if a proper approach has not been initiated. Most alternative health care providers also focus on putting things in. Often it seems that people focus on putting things in, because those who sell products want your business, not your health. If a person cons you into believing they have a superior input product, then they will capture your attention and money. My goal is to set captives free. It is not to get you hooked on a product support system...........The approach focuses on the removal of the primary component in your body blocking your good health. We focus on removal of toxins safely and simply so the products you put in become more effective. With our approach you can greatly decrease the product consumption and multiply their effectiveness at the same time. Removing the blocking agent makes all your input products more effective. Acidic Gas Reconciliation will usher in oxygen and nutrients making all other approaches more successful.

Here is a unique spin on a simple concept. Within this book I will share step one, level one of how to safely, efficiently, and cheaply remove excess CO_2 from the body using common household products. As we move along in future book series I will show you how to target specific conditions and/or produce higher level performance gains as a competitive athlete. I will also release a book on concussions, brain trauma, and mental disorders. Look for "The Concussion Discussion". Ultimately I will cover the simple science behind what I am sharing with you. The science has been around for a very long time, and the ability to understand and utilize it has been around for quite a while. It is simple to understand, but I figured producing healthy results first would make better sense than explaining a foundational component of the universe that you do not know you need to become healthy.

When I was dealing with Whidden's accident and issues there was no one there to help in that time of need. The conventional medical approach seemed to always be to medicate and wait. The neurology approach was so slow and ineffective that it seems they would just medicate until the patient became comfortable with their new medicated self. There seemed little to no effort to restore function.

Here is a critical thought leading into our discussion on oxygenation. If you can stitch the ideas together you now are understanding that CO2 is a waste product generated by the body. There is an accumulation associated with every sickness you have had or ever will have. As a result of environment and culture you have lost the ability to properly regulate oxygenation. You are dying at all times because of CO2 accumulation is unresolved. Now, stop and look at what many Westerners drink. They drink SODA, and fizzy drinks with CO2 loaded in them! It is a waste product your body is already choked by and every energy drink, soda, or carbonated beverage is trying to kill you! Think about it! I will show you how to reconcile this situation. You will see such huge physical, mental and medical relief from our oxygenation approaches through Alkaline Emersion (Acidic Gas Reconciliation)one would hope you would soon put down the fizzy drinks...............Meanwhile, note all those who complain about "phosphoric acid" and "sugar" in sodas, when the most toxic of all is the CO2!! The secret ingredient to these drinks is actually a slow, agonizing death. Meanwhile, those who are "aware" of health have been caught unaware once again. They became so fixed on the fight, they failed to note the most toxic part of soda may be the CO2.

The Western Condition is an umbrella term for all CO2 induced sicknesses. As CO2 accumulates in the tissue it displaces potential for oxygen and nutrition and creates localized acidosis. In so corrupting the cellular environment anaerobic fungus and infection sets in. This action prepares the environment for cancer and virtually every sickness you have or will ever have. This will never change. It has been as foundational to the universe as gravity or the rotation of the earth. I am pleased to be the one to bring it to you saving hundreds of millions of people from cancer, sickness, and auto-immune problems.

1) CO2 is a by-product of every cell in the body.
2) CO2 is a toxic, acidic gas.
3) CO2 handling and management is a full time, continu-

ous job for the body.

4) EVERY SICKNESS KNOWN TO MAN involves a build-up or imbalance in the CO_2 within the body.

5) CO_2 is at the core of every sickness known to man since the beginning of time, and throughout eternity. This has never been different, and will never change.

6) The medical industry and educational industry's failure to properly educate the public on CO_2 and CO_2 management has allowed the proliferation of a wide variety of sickness and disease.

7) Eradication of CO_2 anomalies will likely eradicate most sickness in the human condition.

8) CO_2 is a gas in theory that the body should be rejecting. If the body pH is lower than designed or falters locally or generally then the action of CO_2 removal by the body will be impeded.

9) CO_2, a toxic acidic gas, blocks every action, medication, and oxygenation attempt of the body. If/when CO_2 is present in excess in the body then all attempts to reconcile the body will fail, until reconciled.

10) Use of pain medication can be greatly reduced or eliminated entirely by simple CO_2 remediation.

11) Use of antibiotics and virtually all medication is futile with presence of excess CO_2. Note excess CO_2 is often a result or in combination of poor circulation. If/when a person takes an antibiotic or any medication when pain and poor circulation exists then by definition the antibiotic or medication will fail to go to the area desired, because of the low circulation.

12) CO_2 is a blocking agent for oxygen, nutrition and all healing agents of the body.

13) CO_2 provides "cover" for anaerobic infection allowing anaerobes to live/exist in the low oxygen environment

of the CO2.

14) Removal of excess CO2 would super-oxygenate the body, thus killing all anaerobic infection naturally (without antibiotics), would stimulate oxygenation, nutrition and growth.

15) All forms of treatment, drugs, etc. are wasteful if not accompanied with a CO2 removal/remediation process.

16) All cells of the body produce CO2 as a by-product. Even a child could see that there is no better or more productive place to start at cleaning or feeding the body than to remove CO2 which is the universal blocking agent of all wellness. The medical/educational industry's failure to properly educate people on CO2 remediation at times appears a criminal conspiracy because the need is so abundantly clear. Failure of widespread teaching, implementation, and acceptance indicates that research institutes and groups alleging to be fighting sickness/disease often can miss the forest for the trees. There is simply no better, more efficient, broad-based approach to wellness than CO2 eradication. How/Why have they missed it to now? Why are they/will they fight the obvious?

17) Make note of those who reject or oppose this approach. They may have a special interest in favor of deceiving many.

CHAPTER Eight

Practicing Body Chemistry NOT Medicine

(Are you soaking your feet in baking soda water? In a typical bucket of water one would use a couple of handfuls, or enough to get the pH to 8.5.)

During the process I am going to teach, there is a dynamic shift taking place in a person's body at the chemical level. The process is working to remove acid which is often the opponent to all balance in the body. Inefficiencies in our systems introduced by poor diet, low activity, and a host of issues of our environment snowball to create toxic situations in our systems. The process we introduce does not create the balance, but rather serves to remove the "chaos factor". Acid in the system is a chaos factor, so to speak. Acid in the body breaks down minerals creating a toxic gas in the blood system as well as triggering ineffective utilization of minerals and poor oxygenation.

Simply attempting to mineralize the diet or the body is a difficult process unless the environment is shifted. Wellness comes much, much faster when the chaos factor (acid and/or acidic gas) is managed while the health force (alkaline/minerals) is added.

The Alkaline Emersion (Acidic Gas Reconciliation) process described will help your body vent off gases. The gas you "vent" in the soaking (silver sheen and bubbles) actually acts as an insulator in the body and displaces oxygen and flow in your system. By venting the gas, you run cleaner, smoother, and cooler. It is very freeing to you and your system at all levels. When you follow instructions excess toxic gas from your system will move directly out of your body through your skin instead of through your lungs, and your whole body will see an instant sigh of relief (so to speak). Very effective, simple, safe, and cheap.

Venting toxic gases through our approach removes CO_2, and thus increases oxygenation. All pain goes away when done correctly.

As one progresses in the early days of the emersion solution a number of good things will take place. Many will experience substantial movement of mucus/congestion and an opportunity to clear a lot of garbage from their system. Normally a gas exchange takes place in the lungs where your system absorbs air with the intention to extract oxygen, (while off-gases inert, acidic and toxic gases such as CO_2). As you shift from an acidic system to a proper alkaline, your lungs will expel a lot of flem and mucus. This will effectively expose a lot of acreage or real estate in the lungs to increase absorption and gas exchange. Once the "real estate" for the gas exchange increases the body can naturally and simply take in more oxygen and release gas more toxins. A natural, ongoing cleanse has been initiated very simply. This increase in real estate effectively increases the lung/gas exchange ratios and it is like turbo-charging an engine. Better combustion and cleaner running of the engines we call brain, organs, and body. From the moment you start our emersion/cleansing process you will forever be cleaner inside than you were and continue to operate more efficiently. Done correctly and consistently this cleanse will heal you substantially during the treatment and healing will continue for hours and/or days to come.

The toxic gas removal using our system is much like going to kidney dialysis. In fact, many will find it nearly identically the same, except for it is much safer, cheaper, and easier. No need to allow your kidneys to run down until failure before giving them an assisted approach. Kidney dialysis and availability puts people dangerously at risk, and over time people lose toes, feet, limbs thru the dialysis approach. As you note we start our emersion approach with soaking the feet, because that is usually where dialysis and failures of the body loses the battle. We can save limbs, kidneys, and a host of problematic body issues. Read on.

If and when you are immune suppressed as a result of the CO_2 and acid, there is a short term PLUS to that condition during the recovery phase. We can use this to your benefit............Your system working properly would have tried to overcome the high CO_2/Acid situation. Your system would have produced more red blood cells than you really need because of the poor gas exchange ratio. In essence the condition of your body has your body behaving as if you are at high altitude. Your body does this initially in an attempt to overcome the acidosis issues. This over production of red blood cells will reconcile itself in 40 days! (Your doctor will not likely agree, nor understand. Contact our website/blog for more information, or see our fifth book in the series. www.TheBrainCan.com)

Red blood cells (hemoglobin) are traditionally what carries oxygen in your blood. This means when your body is coming off an acidosis situation you may have elevated red blood cell count and thus ELEVATED O_2 potential. It may last potentially for 40 days. You can/will be near super human for a limited time if you manage it correctly. You may be able to diet/exercise like never before. IF YOU DO then you get to keep it. It is not temporary, but there is a "sweet spot" in your recovery for 40 days that will allow you to make any change you ever wanted to make. Do not cheat. Take advantage because for 40 days you will be turbo charged. If you can boost your system, lose weight, etc. in that time you will be a new you. VERY powerful. I am designing health systems around this sweet spot. Contact us through the website for more information: www.TheBrainCan.com.

I can explain this in depth, but you don't need to know how all this works. You just need to be aware that it can/will happen. Our system will instantly begin removal/reconciliation of all CO_2 buildup issues in your body. This should prove very powerful to those with asthma, cystic fibrosis, COPD, and many breathing/allergy issues. Reconciliation of CO_2 will super oxygenate your body, kill most if not all anaerobic infection, and this super oxygenated situation can be sustained for more than 40 days. You will repeat this process we are laying out for you.

As long as you remain with bad habits and environmental influences you will need to continue the reconciliation. Failure to reconcile systems in your body is what allows cancer to occur. You will be able to make more improvement within 40 days of starting our program than ever before. Do not cheat. Follow through. You may never have an opportunity for as much weight loss and improvement at any other time in your life.

What you will find is we are not practicing medicine. Medicine appears to be a system of taking or concealing poisons to control the masses. What we are doing is practicing chemistry. By shifting the body chemistry, we can do what modern medicine cannot.

CHAPTER Nine

Oxygen Revelation
OXYGEN *versus* OXYGENATION

The purpose of this chapter is to attempt to remove confusion. Simply stated there is a difference between oxygen and oxygenation. Oxygen is the actual gas mixed in air that we breathe. Oxygenation is the effective utilization of oxygen. One without the other is somewhat useless. Unfortunately doctors and medical practitioners often focus on oxygen. The real key to health is effective utilization of oxygen which is oxygenation.

Oxygenation is the key to virtually all good health, and lack of oxygenation is the key to virtually all sickness. Virtually every sickness one can imagine is blamed on something suggesting there is an overage of something or a shortage of something. In virtually all situations if one follows the issues all the way to the end, the root cause of sickness is lack of oxygen. Lack of circulation is merely a lack of oxygen, via the failure of some aspect of the body to provide oxygenation.

Oxygenation in the body is achieved by many approaches. One of the most common methods of oxygenation is called "exercise". Exercise typically increases heat, flow rates, and flow range of fluids within the body, thus oxygenating the body. Doctors will often recommend exercise, such as walking or whatever, but what they really should be talking to their patients about is oxygenation. Oxygenation of the body can be achieved by way of sauna, massage, and a host of other methods. Failure to discuss oxygenation and the need to increase flow amounts and range is a common failure in medical practice. Exercise sounds like work. Oxygenation to increase circulation is a better thing to focus on.

At our retreat we offer an array of systems to stimulate oxygenation. You bring the oxygen and we'll show you how to make it work. Oxygen alone is not the key. Note specifically if you see someone using oxygen generators, oxygen bottles, or any kind of supplied oxygen, understand that this approach is not very effective. It supplies oxygen, but not oxygenation. The key to oxygenation is best applied by the removal of CO_2. If you use supplied oxygen or if anyone you know does, get this book in their hands. This could save their lives. We can increase oxygen uptake and utilization for anyone and everyone using the approach herein and other modified breathing systems.

Often medical practitioners can/will recommend oxygen for some patients. This is good and bad. Without a proper focus on oxygenation the focus on oxygen falls short of the expected return, yet the sale and management of oxygen as a controlled substance is big business. Oxygen at normal atmospheric pressure does not often do that much for a person. At least it could do more if properly or differently administered.

The "bad" is that oxygen management (oxygenation) should be the focus, not oxygen. The oxygen management systems of the body and discussions thereof often involves discussion of hemoglobin; since hemoglobin in the red blood cells carries oxygen. Once the hemoglobin in the blood is full of oxygen at normal atmospheric pressure then the blood/body has as much oxygen as it can handle.

The body regulates hemoglobin production. At high altitudes the body produces extra hemoglobin to grab/carry extra oxygen as an attempt to manage oxygenation. Note, altitude issues are NOT the result of the lack of oxygen. There is plenty of oxygen at altitude. The problem at altitude is PRES-

SURE! Pressure, not oxygen, is the reason for breathing difficulty at altitudes. Common discussion often gets this wrong. The pressure of a gas outside of the body actually has to overcome a number of forces to encourage air/oxygen into the body, lungs, cells, blood, etc. At altitude the body senses an absence of oxygen due to absence of pressure. Over time the body will often attempt to produce extra hemoglobin for those who exist at altitude so the hemoglobin can grab/hold more oxygen....

The reason one has trouble breathing at high altitude is explained by "Boyle's Law". The law states there is an inverse reaction to the size of a gas as pressure changes. Thus the decrease in pressure at altitude allows an increase in the size of oxygen molecules (all gases). As a result the hemoglobin "fills up" sooner due to the increase in size of the oxygen molecule. The body produces extra hemoglobin to carry extra-large oxygen molecules. (This is a rough explanation to save time and space on this subject). Meanwhile the shift in the body often takes about 40 days.

The 40 days required for your body to acclimate and complete the process of acclimation is important. We often hear of sports teams having difficulty performing at altitude. This is a result of absence of pressure and their consequential low hemoglobin relative to what is desirable. Also, we hear of endurance athletes who live/train at altitude prior to performance. If they shift residence within 40 days of their event, then their body can often acclimate. When they return to sea-level there is an advantage due to the excess hemoglobin. The concept of "blood doping" is based on this. A person can go to altitude, live 40 days, build their own excess hemoglobin, then make a blood withdrawal, and later they inject their own blood which was enhanced at altitude. This is considered legal "blood doping" in many instances because it is the performer's own blood. The key is hemoglobin which for a period, if in excess, will grab/hold extra oxygen. Again, it takes about 40 days for the body to reconcile a normal excess or shortage of oxygen according to the body's standards. (There are other reasons athletes get ill. We will reveal the answers to this mystery in future presentations. Stay tuned.)

Proper understanding shows that in all situations high and low altitude there is ample oxygen. If that is true and hemoglobin is really what governs how much oxygen we get, then we need to either focus on the hemoglobin (oxygen carrier) or the utilization of oxygen which is oxygenation. Oxygen is rarely the problem. In fact, a major point to be made is that if 100% oxygen has an effect on you in your normal environment such as making you light-headed (or anything else) then you have a problem, a real problem. Stop and focus on this. IF OXYGEN HAS AN EFFECT ON YOU, in your home environment, then YOU ARE SICK! It is that simple.

Oxygen affecting you at your normal altitude is typically a sign that you could have improper levels of hemoglobin. If you get light headed/euphoric, even slightly then this is a sign that you are on the way to the "Western Condition". You are sick. What a simple diagnostic tool?! If oxygen has an effect on you, then it is not an oxygen problem; it is an oxygenation problem. Oxygenation problems are the root cause of all sickness in the body and is the main issue affecting/allowing cancer and almost all forms of the "Western Condition" to exist. Increasing oxygenation will usually eradicate most sickness. This is one reason "exercise" has long been touted as being something "healthy" people do. Yet, it may not be the exercise itself, but rather the oxygenation that occurs as a result/consequence of the exercise. If you understand this, we have just introduced the simplest diagnostic tool possible, the most complete, and the most accurate. Once a person overcomes the oxygenation situation, they tend to start the eradication of all sickness. It is really simple in many ways. We have just traditionally failed to focus on the root cause of most illnesses.

At this point it is likely possible that some recall that the Whidden recovery in large part came through use of HBOT (Hyperbaric Oxygen Therapy). HBOT increases atmospheric pressure, thus squeezing down air/oxygen molecules. By making oxygen molecules smaller more of them fit in the hemoglobin. As the oxygen is further squeezed down the oxygen molecule is then forced through many other types/styles of cell walls in the body/blood.

The membrane of the plasma rejects oxygen at normal atmospheric pressures. With a slight increase in atmospheric pressure the oxygen molecule is reduced in size/diameter to allow it to fit through the plasma wall of the blood/cell. This allows blood oxygen levels at minimally increased atmospheric pressure to increase 5-20 fold! Since oxygen levels radically increase in the body, then oxygenation by default tends to occur. As a result, HBOT will positively affect most conditions of the body. HBOT is one way to increase oxygenation.

HBOT is a super way to treat the body for a host of issues, however it is rarely used by medical practitioners. Unfortunately, as a result, many people who arrive at a hyperbaric clinic arrive as a last resort instead of their first resort; and the HBOT treatments have to overcome a wide array of medical mistakes leading to the frustration or last ditch effort one has when they approach hyperbarics. In my opinion more people should insist on HBOT..................

One complaint some doctors will give you for HBOT is that if it works as prescribed then you will kill off a host of bad things without knowing which bad things the system killed off. BUMMER! I don't want to make friends with sickness. The problem is revealed that doctors are often obsessed with sickness so they can write something on a chart, to get paid by insurance will often miss the approach to WELLNESS, not sickness. WELLNESS eradicates the possibility of sickness. Who cares if your "sickness" is diagnosed if it goes away, never to return? It is not important for you or yours; it is usually only important to the people who get paid. Increased oxygenation will solve many of sickness issues, and insurance companies would be far better off to understand this sooner and insist on oxygenation training and approaches. It will save insurance companies, employers, etc., billions and billions of dollars once the OXY-GENATION REVELATION catches on.

What happens when the body loses circulation for any reason? At one time there is/was nutrient, oxygen rich fluid circulating then it stops for any of several reasons. What happens? The result is that cellular consumption of oxygen and resources such as glucose take place as flow stops/slows. The result is CO_2 and the waste byproducts of the cellular life cycle. As flow slows or stops these waste products stagnate. Pain and sickness results. If there had been no stagnation or slow flow there would be no pain, and no sickness. Can you see it? Flow slows/stops, oxygen is consumed, and CO_2 is left in abundance. Pain and sickness occur. All we have to do is remove the CO_2. It is replaced with oxygen rich, nutrition rich fluids; and healing begins. Pain goes away. It is really that simple.

The return of circulation, thus nutrition and oxygenation, requires through one means or another that waste products are removed. Unfortunately conventional medical/sickness practice focuses on what can be put "in" to the body. People often focus on what can be put "in" because the product flow allows a commercial enterprise to sell you what they have told you to use to put "in". A better argument can be made for health approaches to focus on what can be removed. Watch this..........

CO_2 is a waste product of virtually every living cell in the body. All healthy and unhealthy cells produce CO_2.

Pathogens often produce CO2. Accurate research will show that CO2 is a waste product involved in every painful situation in the body. CO2 is present in every issue of inflammation. CO2 is a toxic, acidic gas involved in all cellular function and must be removed from the body. Only time will tell, but CO2 and CO2 build up appear to be the root cause/effect of virtually every sickness known to man. CO2 and oxygen cannot co-exist in the body. They simply cannot reside in the same location. As a result presence of CO2 in the body, means the absence of oxygen and LACK OF OXYGENATION! Can you see it? It is not nearly as important for us to focus on putting things "in" to the body as it should be removing things "from" the body. CO2 is that thing that needs to be removed. CO2 buildup is at epidemic proportions in our society and the main symptom of the "Western Condition". The "Western Condition", or CO2 accumulation, appears to be the root cause of cancer, high blood pressure, kidney failure and virtually every sickness known to man. It is so critical and so basic in the function of the body that it seems that every single dull, aching, nagging pain in the body is the result of CO2 build up, and thus the absence of oxygen.

Removal of CO2 usually results in OXYGENATION because oxygen rushes in to the fill the void when CO2 is removed! All pain can be removed from the body when the body's ability to manage CO2 and O2 (oxygen) is enhanced. Only time will tell, but understanding of the simple process of remediating CO2 build-up and oxygenating the body will save insurance companies up to 80% of their payouts on medical claims and long term health. What a huge savings! The coolest part is people's lives are really affected in the right direction when a "health" approach instead of a "sickness approach" is adopted.

Removal of CO2 from the body will make most people pain free in minutes. Continued removal will facilitate a wide array of aids the body while environmental issues that induce CO_2 buildup can be addressed. As time will reveal the environment induced by modern civilization initiates a low oxygenation situation in the body, increasing CO_2 and thus increasing cancers and all forms of sickness. It is all created by modernization. Once it is understood a new health approach geared towards reconciliation of the environment can be developed.

I will be releasing a series of books further developing these concepts and explaining the technical and more scientific supports. I will show how animals in nature recognize issues within their system and how they reconcile it. Once a person becomes more aware of these core universal principles the environment we live in can be properly managed as we regain the ability animals have for sensing what they need. There is huge power in the process, and the recommendations within this book help you to begin the reconciliation process. Understand always that every sickness you have ever had was associated in some way with CO_2 build-up, and every sickness you will ever have will be associated with CO_2 buildup. This is fundamental to the understanding of the body and is as basic to the universe as the study of gravity, and our use of air and water. Only a very naïve or corrupt system would miss or fail to acknowledge and teach these principles.

Begin the health process recommended and tune into future unveiling of the principles. For now, it is best that you get started. You needn't understand it completely before getting the benefit. Your first step could be to begin regular alkaline emersion, clean your digestive system, and do the simple detox process recommended. Note virtually all other detox approaches are trying to sell you a product. Note in each instance they attempt localized oxygenation techniques by pushing a product. Once you understand the core issues, you may no longer be product dependent. The common "health" approach often replicates the pharmaceutical marketing approach to create a dependency. A little learning is a dangerous thing. Get educated and protect your loved ones. Education and medical/health freedom are just a few pages away.

Irrefutable facts on CO_2

1) Virtually all cells in the body produce CO_2.
2) CO_2 in excess blocks oxygen and causes pain.
3) All mental and health conditions involve an imbalance of O_2 and CO_2.
4) CO_2 creates anaerobic environments in the body by blocking O_2.
5) CO_2 is at the core of every localized or generalized acidosis condition of the body.
6) CO_2 accumulation allows/hides anaerobic bacteria and infection.
7) CO_2 gas accumulation is a sign of poor circulation. Poor circulation is at the root of all causes/symptoms of sickness in the body.
8) Acidic Gas Reconciliation in the body would remove excess CO_2 and promote rapid oxygenation and healing.
9) Acidic Gas Remediation/Reconciliation (removal of CO_2 excess) would kill most if not all anaerobic infection in the body.
10) CO_2 remediation should be the first (and repetitive) step of all health approaches.
11) CO_2 accumulation allows fungus, and thus cancer to exist, persist, and flourish.
12) The first step to remediating cancer and all conditions related to acidosis (localized or generalized) needs to involve CO_2 remediation.
13) Without CO_2 (Toxic/Acidic Gas) remediation, ALL other approaches are less effective.
14) Acidic Gas Reconciliation promotes OXYGENATION which is what produces health.

CHAPTER Ten

Buffering:

(Soak feet in baking soda and water solution. Watch for bubbles. Feel a release in your breathing?)

This may be the most important chapter that you need to read and attempt to understand. Conventional medical practitioners often allow patients to be deceived as it relates to the subject "buffering" because they are poorly trained in health, and because the commercial interests behind them do not want you to be aware of the power of "Buffering". Buffering works for and against you at all times.

Buffering is what allows at times, and corrects at all times, certain conditions such as acidosis (localized and generalized) and alkalosis (localized and generalized). These terms may be foreign to you, because as long as others give you the mushroom treatment they control your pain and your destiny. Takes the keys of control out of the hands of others. You can once again be in the driver's seat.

A mixing principle commonly referred to as "Le Chatelier's Principle" describes a mixing of solutions that I call buffering. In essence this principle states that when two solutions mix there is a tendency for the properties of the solutions to meet in the middle somewhere. This is CRITICAL to your health.

As an example of "Le Chatelier's Principle" in action, let's take two solutions. One solution is around about 7.5 pH (Alkaline), and the other solution is around about 6.5 pH (Acid). When we mix equal quantities of the solutions together the result is a new solution that is 7.0 or Neutral pH. Read the example again, because it speaks volumes about your health.

In the example above the first "solution" at about 7.5 pH which could represent your body. The human body is supposed to be at about 7.4 pH otherwise you are sick, very, very sick. Meanwhile the second solution is around about the same pH of Epsom salts or certain types of vinegar. Based on the principle of buffering we see that Epsom salts effectively reduces pH in the body, and thus causes sickness through generalized acidosis. We will cover this later, but as we can see from our simple example, doctors who prescribe Epsom salt use may not understand the body. They will slowly cripple you if you listen to them. Stop seeing that doctor and get him a copy of this book so he quits hurting people.

All solutions in the universe are subject to "Le Chatelier's Principle". It does not matter if you put them in your body, or put them on your body. The electrical charges and/or ions that cause/prevent sickness cross semi-permeable membranes such as skin.

The above reason is why a visit to the beach or a natural spring seems to be invigorating. It really is! The chemistry of the body by way of "Le Chatelier's Principle" has the body's low alkalinity (7.4) trying to mix with presumably the higher alkalinity of the spring/ocean..............Here lies a problem. By the same token that your body attempts to buffer or equalize with a healthy environment, it will also buffer or mix and equalize with a toxic environment.

Here is a problem. Science and dermatology in failing to understand the body and chemistry itself have brought us a host of problems. Common dermatology and cosmetology guides will stipulate that the skin is slightly acidic at or around 6.8 to 7.0 pH or thereabouts. Because of their ignorance and general corruption of industry they make "pH balanced" products that are actually on the acidic side to match the skin.........Meanwhile, they fail to acknowledge that the skin is the largest organ in the body and the acidic nature is the body trying to expel or puke out the acids. By putting products on your skin that are commercial you are fouling up the cleaning process of the body. You are blocking the body's ability to free itself of acids and toxins, and you are making yourself sick. This is much of what leads to cancer. The body is choked. A choked, acidic body is what we call the "Western Condition". You are a candidate for cancers and more because of toxic products, because the toxic products using "Le Chatelier's Principle" actually serve to reduce minerals in the body, and increase acidosis, thereby reducing oxygenation. They are killing us!

The buffering concept works moving up or down the pH scale. Everyone on earth who has ever been sick, or ever will be sick suffered from the same thing, acidosis. Yes, there are a couple of exceptions which we will cover, but even those with "alkalosis" actually are suffering most often from "acidosis" as we shall soon see...... Virtually all conditions relating to food, consumption, decomposition, etc. move from alkaline to acid. Any time a body is said to be "alkaline" is often because some component of the body is failing to properly function. The failing component can be in acidosis mode, thus causing alkalosis. We will deal with this another time.

Acidosis is a condition of the body where RELATIVE to the designed 7.4 pH of the Creator the body is operating at a lower, acidic level. Note 7.0 pH to 7.3 pH is neutral to slightly alkaline, but since we have the concept of buffering we realize that anything coming in contact with the body internally or externally with a pH in these ranges or lower are "relatively" acidic to the body and will tend to pull pH down making us sick. Yes, if you follow your doctor's advice and drink 6-8 glasses of water (the wrong water) you will be very, very sick.

Acidosis can be "generalized" such as those with Fibromyalgia, Lyme disease, last stages of cancer, etc. Generalized acidosis is often a systemic condition, and can be easily reconciled with persistence and consistency. The medical industry has largely ignored this. It only takes a few minutes as we will see by the end of this book. It is cheap, quick, and works. They have failed to properly advise us regarding this principle it seems and instead serve toxic drugs to the population.

Acidosis can be localized (found only in a region of the body) such as conditions of Arthritis, high blood pressure, concussion/TBI, PTSD, or early stages of cancer. Localized acidosis is often the result of a pinched nerve (A chiropractor would call that a subluxation), or some starvation of circulation. Localized acidosis often opens the door for other problems, such as fungus, which cascades into cancer and ultimately generalized acidosis and death.

Localized acidosis can block or impede normal organ function in the body. At times it can impede function of liver, kidney and other organs to a point that they fail to properly operate. This is often the root cause of "alkalosis". Read that again, because doctors often foul this up not understanding the function of the body.

Alkalosis is in many ways the opposite of Acidosis, in that Alkalosis is a problem of the body being too alkaline. Mind you both Acidosis and Alkalosis can be a problem for the body. Meanwhile, the normal function of the body is to take alkaline products in and expel products that are often acidic, thus skin, hair, feces, and respiratory gases are often acidic in nature. Alkalosis can be localized or generalized similar to acidosis. The purpose of this book is to address the Western Condition as it relates to acidosis. Since Acidosis (localized) causes most alkalosis this is the best place to start. The book in this series on Concussions, brain injuries, etc. will cover alkalosis as they are closely related.

To show you how simple this is, let's apply a little eighth grade science/chemistry. When I was in eighth grade or thereabouts we made a simple lead-acid battery as an experiment. We simply took two metal (lead) strips, placed some paper/cardboard between the two strips. We rolled them up with layers of paper/cardboard separately the lead strips. We then submerged the rolled up metals/paper in an electrolytic solution (acid). The solution created an exchange to take place between the two plates by way of ions/electrons jumping across the "semi-permeable" membrane of the paper. In so doing we created electricity/power. Amazingly simple. Read it again, get the picture in your mind.

In the Emersion concept (Acidic Gas Reconciliation) introduced by Ted Whidden we repeat the above experiment very simply. We take an alkaline solution, immerse the human body in the solution. The semi-permeable membrane we will call "skin". The toxins and toxic gases in the body electrolytically shift their acidic (bad) charge to the solution and the body instantly becomes healthier through buffering. It is that simple. In this method we will show you how to reconcile the lungs, kidneys, heart, organs, and body. It is that simple.

What happens when one uses Whidden's Alkaline Emersion approach is the body (a sack of fluids) attempts to mix with a higher pH (alkaline) solution, and the result is the higher alkaline solution "robs" the toxic acidic gas from the body. Yes, waste gas from the body bubbles right out of the skin and oxygen/nutrition rushes in to your tissue behind it. With a little repetition and practice this approach will heal virtually every sickness known to man. Mathea and Whidden's future books will cover a host of conditions this simply treated and likely cured.

Every sickness you have ever had likely started as a localized acidosis. Acid robs minerals. Minerals affect oxygen and oxygenation. This is as foundational to the universe as gravity and rotation of the earth. It has never been different, and it never will. For people to fail to break it down this simply and show you how to treat it there must be some financial incentive for them to keep you in pain and sickness. (The preferred starter solution for most people is a baking soda and water solution to soak in. Be careful, work up slowly. It will cause an instant change. Tune in to our website and blog where we guide people daily through this procedure and others. www.TheBrainCan.com)

Localized acidosis stresses the environment of the body, and through buffering it releases toxins and introduces problems in the body. The fact that often we allow this to remain is what cascades into greater sicknesses, and weak body conditions. Meanwhile, the use of reverse osmosis water (Acidic), microwave ovens (depletes critical minerals), sodas (we ingest CO_2 an acidic toxic gas and other toxins), smoking, junk foods, processed foods, etc. all serve to make and keep us sick. You see these poorly mineralized examples further weaken the body and reduce mineralization. So through our modern conveniences (The Western Condition) we lower the pH of things introduced internally and externally. As a result we produce cancer and health deterioration as a matter of course.

The old adage "garbage in equals garbage out" prevails. The poor mineralization of our foods and products, high acid products in and out of the system, and poor environmental conditions are straining everything in our systems. The system can no longer keep it all in balance. We see things such as "osteoporosis" and Fibromyalgia exist because of generalized acidosis of the body. As a result the body is robbed of minerals. You will see the results of these sicknesses earlier and younger in the population because it is approaching epidemic proportions. One such resultant is cancer. Cancer comes from this problem of low mineralization, acidic conditions. Breast cancer and other such cancers come with excessive use of cosmetology products and poor water quality. (A list of acidic product uses follows near the end of this book. Get "The Chemical Conspiracy" book on "mis-practice".) (Hair conditioners are directly linked to cancers and breast cancer. Get our concussion book to see how this "works".)

The amazing and amazingly simple part about all this is that some 80% of all sickness in the body is a result of poor oxygenation. Poor oxygenation is the result of poor mineralization. Poor mineralization is the result of either poor diet and absorption or environmentally induced acids. Within this book we will show you how to use buffering to super oxygenate and mineralize the system while reducing acidosis. By reducing generalized acidosis and reversing the curse so to speak we will show you how to continue through to isolate and identify localized acidosis and how to manage or remove it. Properly implemented we can reduce all short term breast cancers by half, and reduce them further over the long haul.

We will produce a health increase in 100% of all those who follow our instructions. It is nearly a bullet proof health improvement. It is the simplest, cheapest approach you have never been told. In a follow up book on Brain/Concussion/Mental issues we will tell the "Rest of the Story" and cover how to get the opponent argument in order.

Buffering as a concept is being used against you by product purveyors to make you and keep you very, very sick. Buffering can be used to make you and keep you very, very healthy. The vast majority of products on the shelf today can be tested for pH and you will find the majority of what sick people put in their body is acidic, plain and simple. Their bodies have lost the ability and resources to properly buffer, and they are sick. Once they change this pattern everything will work better............In essence when we look at the "Meth user" (Crystal meth and other chemical drugs) we see an accelerated picture of what acidosis does. Where the before and after photos of Meth use are astounding, the same process of deterioration is happening to you and all those around you, just at a slower pace. People today are more violent, less healthy, and more mentally unstable as a result. It is simple to see. Look at the evening news. Look at the hate, violence and ignorance. Test mental patients, killers, cancer patients, and/or yourself. Acidosis, which is low mineralization, low oxygen, and improper use of buffering (materials inside and outside the body) are present in likely 98% of all cases.

Once again, buffering is the mixing of two solutions with the result of a mid-grade product from the mixing. We will teach you how to create an emersion solution approach that will buffer toxic acidity within the body to bring oxygenation, health and wellness to you and yours.

In respect to alkalosis you cannot use this approach, because acidity is toxic to the body. All use of acids on the skin should be avoided. This includes hand sanitizers, cleaners, Epsom salts, most vinegar products, etc. Using acids to buffer the system will lead to sickness. Meanwhile, we see that Epsom salts and some products have almost a cult following promoting them. Noting personally everyone who ever recommended them to me seem to appear severely out of shape, unhealthy, and a little unstable mentally. People recommending acidic products on the body are dangerous to you. Allow me to explain.

The core of the body is said to be about 7.35 to 7.4 pH. Meanwhile this is science's "average". The average person today is severely sick (hence the Western Condition) and this is likely not a good average as a result, however it is the published acceptable average by conventional science. The body kicks off products such as urine, feces, hair, oils, respiration tends to balance acidity. There are processes that temper this to the best of the body's ability to reconcile these issues. The body uses a host of buffering approaches in its management of the system. Meanwhile, the core of the body is alkaline. The exterior is neutral to acidic, yet relatively acidic to the core. The acidic exterior is the body's attempt to expel more acids. Putting acidic products on the skin/body serves to buffer the skin with toxins. You become sick because of toxic products.

In our approach we show you how to take your exterior (skin) from an estimated 6.8 to 7.0 pH acidic condition, to an estimated 7.8 pH alkaline situation. This actually shifts the body pH and health condition very rapidly. This increases oxygen levels in the skin ten-fold and you will breathe differently. As you walk away from this treatment/approach your body will continue to "buffer" the shift we have made to your exterior. Your body will commence kicking off acids from the organs, and from everywhere inside your body to the exterior and the entire body will begin to breathe better. The entire body will experience increased mineralization instantly, and increased oxygenation instantly, and this will last for quite some time. As you progressively buffer your body properly the body will cleanse itself each time, and you will see steady improvement. In fact, following this process will likely block the ability for cancers to exist, and block them from feeding themselves and damaging your system. You can fight cancer for $1 and be healthier as a result! Hallelujah! (Recommend this cancer approach to your friends.)

Clearly, if you have not been told this before then someone is deceiving you. It is as simple as an 8th grade science project to control good health and eradicate breast cancer, the effect of

AIDS/HIV, ADD/ADHD. Fibromyalgia, and a host of sickness. It appears to me people have been living off of your pain.

As one does a web search for mineral baths, spas, etc., one will see where crooked/quack doctors have written in places such as "Wikipedia" that people once thought that mineral springs and such were medicinal. They write as if it was some kind of old time folk lore. What these smelly sphincters are trying to do is keep you from knowing it works, it always worked, it may be the only thing that worked, and it is required for good health.

Use of water and water products below 7.4 pH actually lower the pH of the body through buffering. You will see that buffering occurs, and every major city with "Reverse Osmosis" water treatment will have an increased crime and lack of health in part due to the relatively acid water. The low oxygenation as a result of slowly wicking out the minerals of the body serve to decrease oxygen to the brain and mental illness and violent crimes will increase. The whole Western World (Western Condition) is sliding off the slope because of failures of municipalities, governments, the FDA (Food and Drug Administration), AMA (American Medical Association), and others to alert people to these situations. Middle Eastern countries, African countries, etc. can trace their crime rates and health rates to this simple issue. (Get a copy of this book in to the hands of your law makers and government officials. They are not being informed correctly. Buy a copy today for your city manager. We are developing solutions for households and government entities. Buy a copy for your doctor, because they are not being properly informed, nor are they properly informing others.)

For those on the real extreme of science fundamentally what we really have is a form of "global climate issues" (global warming) or increase in toxic gases in the human system. The body as a picture of the universe is sick due to toxic, greenhouse gas effects. CO_2 and other build-up gases are the contributing cause and in connection with every sickness known to man, past present and future. Depleting the system of these toxins and allowing the body to return to normal function will not only work towards curing the person totally it will help heal their environment.........As we look at coral cultures, fish habitats, etc. worldwide we see the breakdown outside/near large cities because they are dumping huge amounts of acidic water and run off. Low mineralization of the oceans, is what is causing temperature and localized appearance climatic shifts if they are accurately measured/reported. Low oxygenation and mineralization is what makes the oceans warmer. The illusions and facts concerning climate change are obscured by commercial interests, meanwhile your body has a "climate change" it is combatting. It is localized and generalized acidosis by way of the build-up of greenhouse gases. Our system will remove the greenhouse gas accumulation in the body and heal virtually all sickness effects.

Cancer and all known sicknesses (The Western Condition) are actually a "localized acidosis" contained in a human. Acidosis in the body is largely resultant of too many "greenhouse gases" trapped in the body. Acidosis buildup in the environment is the cause of any real (if there are any) climate change. The effect is the same on both environments as they were both created by the same Creator. Increase acids in the environment, lowers oxygen availability.

(Note: Throughout this book we will be discussing Acid Gas Remediation of the human body. Meanwhile the acidification of the oceans and bodies of water from the human/industrial run off of depleted water is causing what some scientists believe is an alteration to the ocean and environment. What we will find is demineralization of waters entering the ocean and other such areas is lowering oxygenation and thus corals are dying, sea water temperature is rising, etc. If/when man takes on the task of remediating the sickness of cancer by way of the methods recommended here, then the runoff will begin to remediate the oceans which are going through a similar problem. It is not a perfect repair to the oceans, but it is a start. Re-mineralization of the body (human and oceans) is required for proper mineralization and temperature maintenance.) (No, I am not an advocate for "global climate issues". I believe the science of global climate change has been as corrupted as that of cancer research. They have too much to gain commercially from the "scare" to correct the problem.)

Buffering as applied to the human body takes several forms. In some instances the body is overloaded or senses too much of something to buffer it. As an example let's look at laxatives. Either an alkaline based or acid based laxative is designed in part to give the body too much of something at once. The body senses that it cannot properly "buffer" the product so it opens the poop chute and lets it pass through. This is one means your body uses to avoid buffering. In the old days your granny might tell you to drink prune juice. Prune juice is highly acidic. In large amounts your body will reject the effort to buffer (opting to maintain your minerals instead) and it will blow through you. Another example is Epsom salts. Epsom salts are extremely toxic inside or outside your body. I can't stress this enough. Fire anyone from your life that recommends use of Epsom salts. Meanwhile, Epsom mixes with water at about 6.4 pH. This is a level to which your body will not try to buffer and will reject it, thus opening the poop shoot and letting it go. This should tell you something about Epsom. Meanwhile, let's take another view. If you were to take an alkaline based laxative it would load your system up with more mineral than your body can properly buffer, and it would reject it and open the poop chute. Meanwhile, focus on this, the alkaline was more "like" you as you are supposed to be alkaline. I would recommend only alkaline based laxatives, and would recommend at this time in your reading of this book you take one. We are going to start cleaning your system and getting you ready for things to come. An alkaline laxative is the first step to wellness for most people. Go ahead, test your system's ability to "buffer". Two to three teaspoons of baking soda in some water should do. Give it a try.

The sicker you are the more alkaline laxative it may take. Think about it. If you are highly acidic, then some of the mineral is going to be absorbed. You can buffer too much when you are sick. Keep an eye on this, because we may be able to use the amount of laxative required (your buffer reaction) to determine just how sick you are.

Do you recall the earlier chapter on MRI (Magnetic Resonance Imaging)? The Magnetic Image or Resonance Differential is formed in the body because of the absence or inability of the body to properly buffer. What happens in the sick body is there are greater and lesser accumulations of metals such as iron due to acidosis issues. If/when we set the stage for the body to be properly alkalinized the dissimilar charges electrically between the new alkaline you and the old localized acidosis then the magnetic anomaly is pulled apart. The accumulation of iron is recirculated/dissipated and we starve the fungus, infection, cancer, or whatever pathogen depends on that environment. Through buffering using an emersion solution we first clean and free the skin (the largest organ in the body), then we incrementally clean and address each organ within the body as we continue the process. Once the body is thoroughly cleaned and proper balance restored the overall "charge" of the body electrically is far stronger than the concentration of charge at this sick or affected area. The body pulls apart the electrical anomaly and in so doing will serve to starve/kill the cancer, fungus, problem, etc. As we continue the body gets stronger and stronger and pathogens, and such get weaker and weaker.

It does not require medication or anything harmful. Meanwhile, if you are taking medication for infection or anything else, you must understand that anomalies within the body shown on an MRI are typically blood flow irregularities. If you have blood flow irregularity then by definition there is often low/no flow. The medication will not get there, because you lack circulation. Meanwhile with our approach we stimulate total body reconciliation. Our approach will help carry medications throughout the body.

What you must understand is that buffering is happening throughout your body at all times. One of the main (only?) causes of cancer is a failure of your body locally or systemically to buffer, OR it is the body's correct use of buffering, yet you are ingesting and immersing yourself in the wrong products. Can you see it? What studies will show is the incidence of cancer and sickness is higher in high population dense areas and areas with use of acidic water such as "Reverse Osmosis" water. The gradual draw down or reduction of minerals through buffering using toxic products takes its toll. It drains the body of electrolytic resources, and drains and drains. Meanwhile taking supplements will not sufficiently overcome this. You must stop the improper draining by exterior forces. Our water in many areas these days is toxic by way of processing. People put water softeners on their systems to remove minerals when you NEED THOSE MINERALS! Use of mineral depleted products on or in you will kill you.

As you begin to look at your water and other such products understand you really "Are what you eat". You are actually what you bathe in as well. Buffering of the toxic products are causing likely causing breast cancer and every form of cancer and sickness. STOP!

Buffering improperly is a main factor in why athletes get cancer. The classic runner who runs 5 miles a day yet gets cancer is a result of running in the rain (acid at times), sweating (acid at times), working out (CO_2 and toxic build-up), and a host of self-inflicted problems without using buffering afterwards to "wick away" the poisons. Yes, they can do everything correct, but if they shower in Reverse Osmosis or other mineral depleted water they will get weaker and weaker. The body's inability to buffer or create mineral opens the door for the cancer. (There are other reasons why athletes become sick/weakened. We will cover this in future presentations. Stay tuned.)

Understand that the BODY DOES NOT CREATE MINERAL. When wackos tell you something is "Mineralizing". Ask yourself, "Where does the mineral come from?" If folks tell you an acidic drink/product is "Alkalinizing", then you must understand it is likely robbing minerals from somewhere such as your body, because it is acidic and that's what they do. This is buffering working against you because you have been misinformed. This is why over the long haul people following this advice will become sicker. You must understand practitioners often mislead you out of their own ignorance, and as long as you are crippled or partially wounded they get to sell you more product. Remove these toxics acids from your world, and you will see an instant resurrection of services in your body. We will show you an example that will completely shift your body in less than 5-10 minutes from beginning the test. You will like the results. (In an alkaline emersion soak, try to get in as large a body of water as practical. We have found that in a 100 gallon tank wherein the volume of water is 3x times the human body that a better exchange takes place. Imagine a more powerful force outside of your body at 8.5 pH pulling at three times the combined power on the things in your body (toxic gases) that your body wants to reject. Greater bubbling and gas exchange takes place it seems.)

Buffering properly raises the pH and in so doing lowers acids in the body. Acids in the body rob minerals. Minerals promote oxygenation, so removing more acids, more effectively will make you instantly stronger, sharper, etc. Over the short and long haul your body moves in a direction of either mineral depleted, or minerally balanced. Since most of our foods are processed, they lack proper minerals. Since many of our foods are microwaved, they lack proper minerals. Since much of our processed water is lacking minerals we seem to be getting depletion from all sides............What we will show you is how to deplete the acids. Depleting the acids, will shift the tide, boost the minerals and you will be happier and healthier instantly. Watch and see.

As you will see "Buffering" takes place all around you every day. Buffering problems are at the root of every sickness and every health breakthrough you can/will ever have. By using buffering to your advantage in Ted Whidden Alkaline Emersion (Acidic Gas Reconciliation) Approach you will quickly be able to thwart virtually all sickness. Buffering is powerful to understand. Buffering is powerfully working against you if you do not understand it, so tune in. We will teach you how to create a solution at home to reconcile your sickness issues. We will provide a website and blog to keep you up to date on the amazingly simple solutions to fighting cancer and all sickness. www.TheBrainCan.com

(Whidden proofread this part of the book. Repetitive indeed, but not bad for a guy who one lost 94% of brain function. Read on.)

Buffering facts:

1) Le Chatelier's principle indicates that all solutions when mixed move towards the middle of physical characteristics of those fluids used in combination.

2) The human body is a moving sack of chemical solution and electrolytes.

3) The human body as a sack of solution continues to assimilate and take on characteristics of its environment.

4) The human body when immersed in a solution will attempt to "normalize" with the solution by way of Le Chatelier's principle.

5) If/When the human body comes in contact either internally or externally with acids or oils it tends to lose or give up minerals and thus loses mineralization.

6) Loss of mineralization as we have seen in previous chapters causes a loss of oxygen and oxygenation.

7) If/when the human body comes in contact with alkaline of a nature stronger than the body (relative alkalinity) then the body loses ACIDS and acids gas to the mineral solution!

8) Immersion of the human (mammalian) body in an alkaline solution at 8.5 pH (or relatively alkaline) will cause the CO_2 and toxic acidic gases in the body to be INSTANTLY wicked out of the body and in to the solution, thus soaking in a baking soda water solution would effectively remove excess toxic gas from the body, instantly oxygenate the body, kill anaerobic bacteria, and promote general wellness in the human body. There is no faster, cheaper, more efficient, more effective, or more universal application approach available to mankind. (It has simply not been shared with the public, because it is so universally successful, cheap, accessible, and does not need a doctor's prescription.)

9) Since CO_2 is produced by every cell of the body, and since it is the universal blocking agent to all wellness of the body there is no better place to start when cleaning up or preparing the body.

10) CO_2 remediation has universal application potential for solving/addressing all health problems of mankind.

11) The emersion approach works for or against all individuals all the time irrespective of whether they are aware or not. Use of toxic water and products on the skin creates sickness. Use of healthy products as outlined and recommended herein will promote health.

12) We will find that poor product and environmental design and implementation is what causes or allows cancers by misuse and/or misapplication of Le Chatelier's principle. The use of most cosmetic products degrade the human condition, lowering mineralization and thus oxygenation of the body. The lack of understanding of this principle allows cancer and other sicknesses to perpetuate. (See "The Chemical Conspiracy" book.)

13) If anyone anywhere was really researching methods to improve the body condition and create cures then someone would have presented this before now, AND made it a universal approach.

14) If anyone anywhere was really trying to treat or cure anything, they would tell you about this simple approach.

15) You need to get a copy of this book in to the hands of each or your friends, family members, and medical personnel with whom you are connected.

CHAPTER Eleven

Bubble Diagnostics

Bubble diagnostics is a powerful yet simple topic to cover, yet very important to address. As you have or will see an Alkaline Solution of about 8.5pH or higher will cause bubbles to form in the water when you immerse your body in it. EVERYONE will ALWAYS make bubbles. A problem will likely exist because in the early days your perception of bubbles will mislead you. You simply do not know what to look for, yet everyone makes bubbles.

The reason some will not perceive bubbles is simply being oblivious to the effect. Everyone around you has likely always been oblivious so not to worry. Now that you are aware, look for them. Half or more of the "bubbles" or gas exiting the body will mix in to solution so you will not "see" all the bubbles, so any presence of bubbles is a good sign and a positive effect.

The bubbles which come from the body consist of toxic gases. In fact, they are toxic acidic gases your body if functioning correctly would get rid of anyway. The fact that they are toxic, acidic means they need to go. The presence or existence means you had an excess. Everyone will bubble given proper conditions whether you recognize or acknowledge the bubbles or not. This is crucial to understand. Your lack of observation skills and those you know will fool you. It has fooled millions of people for thousands of years, because someone, somewhere should have discovered this and presented it before now. In fact, anyone sincere in a health pursuit would have stumbled across this over and over again.

The bubbles formed in an 8.5 pH of greater alkaline solution needed to go. This is true in all respects. Your body was preparing or getting ready to remove them, but for a number of reasons your system failed. This failure is associated with every systemic condition of the body. The accumulation of bubbles in the system is epidemic and an indication of sickness.

Meanwhile, in lieu of MRI scans, Pet-CT, and all these scans, all one needs to do is immerse the person/patient in an alkaline solution and look for bubbles. The bubbles will always come from an accumulation of toxic gases. The pain in the region will "bubble away", because the toxic gas is clearly the place holder which prevents oxygen and oxygenation from being present. Once the toxic gases depart then a "siphon" of sorts forms and the removal of toxic gas through the skin will effectively "wick in" or siphon oxygen and nutrition in to the space where the toxic gas was. Health and nutrition is instantly boosted. In so doing, the oxygenation shift will begin killing off anaerobic infections of all kinds. By definition the admission of oxygen to the body will kill the anaerobes safely and effectively.

The bubbles will not only help diagnose the location and nature of the problem, but it is therapeutic as well. Healing takes place while the information is gathered. The effects are immediate and undeniable, however people have dumbed down their senses to things of nature. You will need to repeat this numerous times to get a full grasp and understanding. A host of changes will take place.

Have you ever heard of someone who had a "trick knee" or some other joint pain or issue that helped them "predict the weather"? We hear of this all the time where old people say they can tell a storm is coming because of joint or bodily discomfort or stiffness. Why is this? If you knew would you do something about it? Would you tell people? Would you share this book?

The joint discomfort, trick knee or whatever that allows those with injuries to predict weather are actually the sign of high CO2 and low oxygen. This should be remediated. In fact, if not remediated when it happens then the conditions of the body get progressively worse. Weather prediction using joint/body discomfort is the sign of a potentially dangerous condition.

As we discussed previously and elsewhere the body senses atmospheric shifts. The bodily reaction to atmospheric pressure shifts is directly explained by Boyle's Law which indicates the volume of a gas is inversely proportional to the pressure on the gas. In short, if you double the pressure on a gas, you have half the volume. If you reduce the pressure by half, then you double the volume.

What happens with low atmospheric pressure is the size of oxygen molecules "grows" a bit due to the loss of pressure. (Loss of pressure, increase in volume.) When the size of oxygen molecules "swell" from the absence of pressure then your hemoglobin which carries oxygen "fills up" faster. It thus carries fewer oxygen molecules, and thus an oxygen starvation is initiated. What you experience is an absence of oxygen and oxygenation as a result, and consequently a build-up of CO2, because of poor circulation at the old injury sight............This should tell you that you need to immediately do an alkaline immersion. This will draw out the excess CO2 and toxic gases, super oxygenate the area, and as a result once the storm passes you will be in better shape than you would be otherwise. Your recovery will be much faster, and you will see greater life, and less death in your system.

Note emergency rooms, health care clinics, etc. when storms pass. Those places fill up because of the boost in anaerobic issues as explained above. It is big business for them. Take that opportunity away from them. Buy some baking soda and start healing your family.

People with wounds that allow them to predict weather must come to understand that there is a level of starvation that takes place each round. The oxygen deprivation that takes places allows anaerobes (infection) to set up and re-commence their dirty work. It does not have to be this way. You can super oxygenate as often as you wish using Ted Whidden's Alkaline Emersion process for removing toxic gases.

The bubble diagnostics will vary subtly with conditions. The key is to push/test for 8.5 pH. Do not exceed 9.0 pH otherwise it could "burn" you (Caustic burn). If it does "burn" slightly this too shall pass. In each situation you will see bubbles. You will see specifically where your problem is. It is not "symptom" focused but CAUSE focus. The medical industry may reject this approach because once you find the true cause and the peripheral issues of CO_2 accumulation and reconcile it then you will be far healthier. In fact, many people see their symptoms dissipate while nutrient and oxygen flows properly and true healing begins.

There is often a "cascade effect" of problems connected with a sickness. There is a general deterioration that follows a specific deterioration. This approach treats it all the same and for the first time full body reconciliation takes place.

Once one discovers the actual location of their core issue then one can make a poultice of baking soda and borax, wet the poultice and place it on/near the injury or problem. This will help, but not address the generalized acidosis condition of the body. This approach is used for localized acidosis which is where sickness begins. Washing the entire body in an alkaline solution following use of the poultice will promote a generalized healing following the specific area treatment. It is always recommended to use a general soak with the use of a poultice.

In each case one can monitor the bubbles being released to know if their problem is increasing or decreasing. With each immersion the body is healed to a level and can continue to heal for up to 12 hours. Many/most of the conditions of the body are environmentally induced by way of abuses over time. In essence your deterioration is a process. If a process caused or is causing your problem then it will likely take a process to treat the problem. As long as a person continues questionable lifestyle approaches then they will have to likely continue the treatment. Meanwhile, virtually everything in a modern world seems engineered in a manner that failed to take in to consideration the principles presented within this book. As a result virtually everything you do is unhealthy by design. Use of conventional products, foods, and lifestyles is actually considered questionable lifestyle because mankind has moved so far off the true path to health.

In our example with Mr. Whidden, we effectively used Bubble Diagnostics and therapy more than 3 ? years after his accident to find and resolve issues that MRI, Pet-CT and all wide array of sophisticated testing could not resolve. Meanwhile, this costs only pennies, can be done daily, in the privacy of your home. It is a far superior way to check on and remediate your condition.

The way bubble diagnostics works is simple enough an 8th grade science project can test it. The acidic gas in the body "pockets" or stagnates in poorly served tissues of the body. The body would reject the gas normally if the region was better served. This toxic gas if handled correctly would in part be shifted to the lungs where an air/gas exchange takes place. Yet if the gas is not mobilized from the injury or problem area then it resides. While it resides it blocks oxygen. Blocking oxygen allows or causes pain. Anaerobic infection sits up in the area, and general sickness of the body is on the horizon. The solution of water for immersion mixed at 8.5 pH has a ten times greater "strength" than that of a normal body at 7.4 pH. The sick portion of the body is most often lower than 7.4 pH due to low oxygenation, low mineralization, etc. The "solution" in your body attempts to normalize with the solution you are immersed in just as predicted by Le Chatelier's Principle. The toxic gas in your body which would normally be rejected is promptly ejected straight through the skin in to the immersion solution. The reason this happens is the electric charge of the solution at 8.5 pH and your sick areas of the body oppose one another. Opposites attract. The solution's "pull" on your sick, acidic gas is greater than that of your body, so your body let's go, and great healing takes place. Your toxic gas goes right out in to solution, thereby making bubbles. The bubbles you make in the water are clearly not needed as you will see body function improves substantially with each round.

The solution will actually shift the pH of the skin to more alkaline making if softer and smoother. You will not need lotions and products because your body will take care of this. Your body internally will shift acids to the outside cleaning the interior, and preparing for your next soak. With each round you will increase life with the Living Waters of the solution.

Baking soda is often recommended for making solution in the beginning because baking soda will limit the pH shift in the solution to a very safe 8.5 pH.

As you continue your lungs will clear and your ability to more naturally manage $O2$ and $CO2$ on a daily basis will increase. You will become substantially healthier as a result. It will work for everyone you know.

People with asthma will bubble bodily and immediately recognize better breathing. Same for cystic fibrosis, COPD, fibromyalgia, etc. You see a condition common to all sickness is $CO2$ excess from poor bodily function. $CO2$ is produced by every cell of the body, so beginning with $CO2$ remediation is fundamentally important, and there is no better place to begin in many instances. The fact that the medical community have missed this should raise suspicions.

CHAPTER Twelve

Capacitor/Condenser Theory

As it regards Cancer, Breast Cancer, Immune Deficiency Issues, AIDS/HIV, Fibromyalgia, ADD/ADHD, and a host of problems with sickness in the human body it seems irresponsible for us to think that professionals in the medical field will develop cures. There are a number of reasons for the corruption and incompetence we can expect to find. Mainly there is likely peer pressure and financial gain NOT to find a cure. As we seek help for sickness in the USA and beyond notice most often we are given "treatment" and not a "cure". The treatment often chases symptoms rather than causes. As long as you chase/treat symptoms, rather than curing causes people will remain sick, and the medical industry will remain expensive (and ineffective). People profit off of your pain and sickness.

One of the reasons for medical industry inefficiency is training. Training at times blocks the creative process of the mind. If you are enamored by corrupted science and overwhelmed with details, special interests, and commercial incentive there is little reason to look outside for answers. Oddly the public is abnormally enamored by the American Medical system, when in fact we have explained simply a number of fundamental, foundational health issues leading to this point that you did not know, nor did they apparently know. Are you pleased with the mushroom treatment you have been getting? They are keeping you in the dark on simple health concepts. See "The Chemical Conspiracy" book that uncaps the well of misinformation in the medical business.

What if I told you the answer to cancer and most Western illness would come from outside their industry? Would you be willing to consider a simple answer has been before our eyes all along, yet the "professionals" have missed it either because of improper training and understanding or lack of incentive to explore a path to cure?

As we established previously using the chapter on MRI (Magnetic Resonance Imaging) the body is full of soft metals. In fact if this were not true then the concept of MRI would not work. It measures magnetic anomalies within the body which is based in variations in soft/medium metals within the body. It is that simple. Meanwhile, we can see that the envisioning, designing, developing, building, maintaining, and operating the MRI machine is actually far more complicated than treating the problem once you know it is there. Here is a key. The development and marketing of MRI technology is actually infinitely more complicated than just treating the magnetic anomaly in the body. Once you resolve the magnetic anomaly within the body, the conditions for sickness often go away and the person gets well. Meanwhile, industry chose to build and market a system for "imaging" sickness, rather than using the same technology to END the sickness. It is all a commercial game, whereas people profit off of your sickness and pain. Can you see this? Hopefully you soon will. We will solve this equation and give you the answer.

So, we have metal and magnetic anomalies in our body that show sickness. Seems simple. The technology is readily accepted today.

Meanwhile during our discussion on buffering we discussed "Le Chatelier's Principle" where solutions tend to mix to form a mid-range solution with characteristics of each solution. It can be reasonably established that in the mixing of solution to bring about this principle that ions and/or electrical charges shift from one part of the solution to the other. For the pH of a solution to shift there are thousands of tiny electrical exchanges.

We discussed oxygen and oxygenation. We discussed that if/when oxygen flow is deprived to a part of the body then the nutrient rich (minerals/metals) and oxygen in the blood/fluids stop or slow flow. We discussed that as the oxygen flow slows that oxygen dissipates from the fluid leaving CO_2 and other toxic gases from that combustion action in the cell. Here is where our problem develops. This is too simple to miss so read this carefully.

Acidic gases and fluids within the body consume soft metals. Soft metals consumed by acidosis in the body generally cause systemic failure and lowering of oxygen in the system. Lowering of oxygen in the system occurs in part because the toxic gases which are not flowing out or being flushed from the low flow area block the resurrecting power of oxygen.

Soft metals in acidic solution form a BATTERY! An electric battery is a collection of soft metal plates in an acidic solution. Look at the 12 volt "lead-acid" battery in your car. It is exactly the same. The more acids and metals the stronger the battery. The stronger the battery and acids, the less oxygen in your system. Locally this is what we call "pain". If you can dissipate the acid then most pain goes away. Now, it is/was a process for you to build up an acid imbalance in the system. It will take a process to relieve it.

Meanwhile, the lead-acid battery we have mentioned several times in this book is a perfect image of how the body operates in decline. Notice your car battery is plastic so that the outer cover does not conduct electricity. The isolated sack of acidic fluid with soft metals in it creates and stores enough electrical charge to start your car repetitively for years with low/no additional inputs. It receives a charge slowly from the alternator on your car, but has "CCA" (Cold Cranking Amps) to really give it a boost to start and run........Okay, your body is no different.

Look at your body in a new way. You are nothing more than a sack of electrolytic solution with soft metals in it. You are very much designed like a common lead acid battery. The core difference is that you are designed to operate at around 7.4 pH. Yet, we have demonstrated that all your skin care products, water, products you ingest, etc. have been systematically depleted over the recent years of development. We see that microwave ovens deplete essential minerals. We see that water where once pure and super mineralized has been reduced to an acid through "water treatment", reverse osmosis, bottling, etc. Meanwhile if/when your body becomes low mineralized then you become a more acidic bag of minerals.

Acids within our system in low circulation areas easily take over a region. They consume soft minerals (potassium, magnesium, calcium, etc.) and trace minerals. (I think trace minerals missing tend to cause more problems than one can imagine). What they are left with often is iron as it is one of the last to be consumed. The concentration of iron in a weak acidic solution creates an electric field which in turn the iron becomes magnetized! Hence the MRI (Magnetic Resonance Imaging) actually takes a picture of the built up iron reserves from localized acidosis. Hallelujah! Meanwhile, it would only cost about $1 to dissipate the iron/acid condition and end the problem. Difficulty is no one would make money off of solving the problem. They had rather image it.

Follow this. I am about to share with you something that no one knows. The system explained above is how cancer "feeds" itself. Pay close attention, because if you can learn how something feeds or sustains itself, then you can discover how to control it. This is a Nobel Prize kind of release!!

The iron in acidic solution with other metals creates a capacitor/condenser type situation in the body. (A capacitor is an electricity storage device.) The electricity surrounding the metal creates MAGNETISM! Magnetism is what the MRI measures. MEANWHILE, Cancer in the body is a rogue pathogen. It must somehow draw resources to it for a feeding mechanism. In tests from the 1970's they have demonstrated that cancer cells on the eye-ball of a rabbit would somehow "draw" blood through blood vessels to it for feeding. How can it do this? Very simply via MAGNETISM!! Seriously! The soft metals in acid create electricity. Electricity in metals creates magnetism. The magnetism in the localized acidosis creates a magnetic pull. The magnetic pull attracts the iron in the blood/fluid. Iron in the blood is found in hemoglobin so it slowly robs resources from the fresh blood of body. The by-product of the cancer's action and acidic consumption is more acid. The more acid the stronger the "battery" becomes. The stronger the battery becomes the stronger the "magnet" becomes. The stronger the magnet, the faster the cancer feeds. The faster it feeds, the more resources lost and the more acid/acidosis.

Localized acidosis leads to a more generalized acidosis and the body shows signs of sickness. Generalized acidosis robs minerals, thus oxygen from the body, and eventually the kidneys give out and death results. Amazing, yet amazingly simple. MRI concepts teach that if anyone was truly seeking the answer surely they would have figured this out by now.

Now, all we have to do is dissipate the original problem (acidosis) through proper buffering and the initial buildup cannot occur. Even better than that. If we use buffering correctly we can coax the body to buffer in an emersion solution, then the exterior of the body is "different" than before. For 12+ hours after emersion the body will continue the buffering/equalization process with the skin. The skin will help balance the body. You must understand the skin by way of our toxic environment has been dissipated of minerals. We can use a similar process to dissipate acids and acidic gases from the body. A near instant pain relief will occur and overall shift in body chemistry. Over a simple, short process the body can be completely reconciled. As the body is reconciled generally the body itself will begin to reconcile "localized" acidosis issues. The localized acidosis which is the root of cancer and every sickness known to man (The Western Condition) will be destroyed through buffering when the body is properly balanced.

In applying proper buffering techniques through Ted Whidden's Alkaline Emersion (Toxic Gas Reconciliation) approach virtually all sickness in the body leaves. Complete reconciliation of any/all issues takes place which reverses the curse of the Western Condition. As the skin is the largest organ in the body we use it as a contact point for diffusing the excess electricity (acidosis) in the body. There is an instant power boost from increase in oxygenation. Further as acid is actually removed instantly from the body, the mineralization of the body instantly increases, with better absorption and retention of future meals and minerals because there is a reduction in the acids and acidic gases that have been robbing minerals. There is an exponential shift in healing as these things radically work to return the body to a condition of health.

As it regards cancer (and all other sickness) buffering with Whidden's Acidic Gas Reconciliation approach can kill it simply. The removal of toxic waste from the area slows the cancer growth substantially. You see the waste product from the cancer is acidic and generates the "power" for it to feed. Remove it and it begins to starve. Meanwhile the waste from the cancer is a neurotoxin. It's "puddling" in and around the cancer is what kills tissue around the cancer giving the cancer a chance to grow unrestricted. By dissipating the neurotoxin the body resists the unrestrained growth of cancer. By dissipating the neurotoxin the acid/battery/electricity/magnetism feeding cycle of the cancer is broken and it begins to starve. By shifting the body chemistry radically to a more alkaline situation using emersion the strong dissimilar charges between the "localized acidosis" (cancer) and the generalized alkalosis of the body, the acid loses to the greater charge and power of the alkaline body and the electrical charge, acids, battery, electricity, and magnetism of the cancer/sickness is destroyed. The body actually now has the power to overcome and eject the cancer just like the body would reject a foreign object like a wood splinter. The body will squeeze the cancer down, starve it out, and will at times force masses to the surface of the skin. The mass will be reduced as it moves to the surface, and at best the only future for cancer research/doctors is to remove the remnant when it reaches the surface of the skin. (Inoperable cancers can be quickly, simply, and safely reduced as well, using a generalized and localized reconciliation approach. See the website www.TheBrainCan.com.)

The technique recommended should extend the life and quality of life for all cancer patients. Properly implemented it would eradicate any/all possibility of future cancers.

Cancer is a problem we as humans have "cultivated". We have changed the "soil" chemistry of our body and all the products we input and use. In so doing we have altered the body chemistry through unhealthy environment to actually cultivate and grow cancer. All we need to do to eradicate cancer is to shift our body chemistry back to how it was designed to be. We can do this immediately through Alkaline Emersion (Acidic Gas Reconciliation) techniques. There is no better, faster, or more effective means to do this.

Virtually all sickness in the body follows this basic pattern. People want to think their sickness is special or that there is something elite in having a diagnosis. Virtually all sickness in the body comes through oxygen deprivation. Oxygen deprivation comes with CO_2 buildup. CO_2 buildup can be reduced through simple Alkaline Emersion (Acidic Gas Reconciliation) eradicating 80% of all infectious issues, almost all pain, restoring oxygenation, and removing almost all symptoms.............Uniquely when we remove the underpinnings and symptoms of sickness properly through this method then very often the rest of the body resumes normal function and all sickness tends to leave the body..........If you have some injury or issue that permanently starves or tends to starve an area then you have sickness that has been in process. If you have a process working against you, then implement a process to thwart that degradation. In our example of Ted Whidden, following his accident he had a recurring theme in his sickness. What he did was develop a process to overcome this systemic deterioration. In so doing, aspects of his immune function returned which was a big plus. Many other issues were self-resolved. Without medication he was able to begin to resolve and manage his issues. In experiments we had 100% success in improving people irrespective of their diagnosis or condition. Reconciling acidosis and stray electrical issues (and thus magnetic anomalies) actually solves most all problems of the Western Condition.

The key to changing the electrical/magnetic characteristics of the body is as simple as taking a bath in a balanced electrolyte solution. Didn't I tell you it was simpler to solve the magnetic resonance issues than to image it? It is. Someone has been hiding secrets from you.

Another reason why cancer research continues going nowhere is because of improper training, motivation, and understanding. It is a simple electrical problem. (Here comes another Nobel Prize winning idea!) The cancer cells act as little capacitors storing power as we discussed earlier with acidosis with metals in it. As the cancer cells reproduce you have a cluster of cells. This cluster of cells acts as if they are capacitors in parallel. Electrical capacitors in parallel all have a small power draw separately, but in a cluster they join forces and there is an exponential electrical/magnetic "pull". As the mass grows it feeds faster and faster because the power of the cells working as a parallel circuit. The electricity increases, as does the acidity, as does the magnetism, until it overwhelms the area and the host. Generalized acidosis and neurotoxins kill the host often resulting in kidney failure...........As the kidney failure is the ultimate demise of the host, we use a system to build up kidney function and completely reverse this process. Astoundingly simple, fast acting, and CHEAP!!! You want to tell your friends to read this book. Cancer is simple as can be

The beauty is that all these answers are clearly before us. The approach to reconcile body chemistry is simple, straight forward, and an eighth grade science student should be able to understand it. Meanwhile, you needn't understand it. Just do it, as they say. Just do it and share this book with others. (Nike and other athletic sponsors should step forward before our next book release!)

Oddly if you follow the body is a sack of minerals in an electrolytic solution then you see can see that if it is left "ungrounded" then electrically the charge builds up and is stored like that of a capacitor. The build-up and anomalies is what induces and allows cancer to continue. Diffusing the power through our Acidic Gas Reconciliation plan should change (and greatly improve) how cancer is fought.

Spread the word, we can reduce all forms of breast cancer quite quickly for only a few dollars on locally acquired bath products. It is simple, really. The only difficult part is to reach those in need. Please help.

CHAPTER Thirteen

Short Breathing

Most people in our culture fail to breathe properly. Very few INHALE deep enough or often enough deeply. When we feel pain we exhale, when we get frustrated we exhale. When do we inhale? Inhale deeply several times. Continue doing this throughout your day. Now, soak your feet in baking soda water solution and purposely breathe in deeply, often.

Mankind simply gets it wrong much of the time. We short breathe or fail to properly inhale good air, and fail to exhaust the bad. It is really simple to get wrong, yet very simple to get right. Why are you doing it wrong?

So many of you are wondering, how can this be? How can we be so far removed from what is correct in our culture? How can seemingly healthy people, people who exercise get cancer, and sickness? How can this be happening?

The answer to these questions is simple actually. Man and mankind are working towards the death and end of its own existence and destruction of the world. Man is at the helm of his own demise. This has been known since the beginning of time. Even the Holy Bible says that that "Mark of the Beast" 666 is the number of MAN! Man is the problem. Watch and see.

Look at the bottoms of your feet, the palm of your hands. Now look at your pets paws. Do you see any "real" difference"? Many of our pets have padded feet just like humanoids. These padded feet are supposed to impact the ground. In fact we use the term in electricity of "grounding" a device to complete a circuit. The human hand/foot is designed to impact the ground and electrically diffuse excess electrical charge. The use of shoes began the decline of mankind because we lost contact with the earth. Early shoe designs used natural materials and developed to use metal tacks or nails in them. These shoes were not so bad, but sickness increased. Today's shoes are completely synthetic with rubber soles that prevent any form of contact with earth. As a result of wearing fully insulated, rubber shoes we lost the contact with the earth that diffused excess electrical.

Accurate study will show that cultures who wear shoes have a far higher incidence of cancer than those who don't. I know there are lots of wacky fish oil studies and other crap about heart/cancer issues. These are put on by people who sell fish oil. Meanwhile, those cultures who consume fish oil also work the ground, are barefooted, or exposed to the ocean. They are electrically more balanced as a result. That is the connecting aspect of their life. Everything else appears a hoax to sell you a product. The cure/connection is likely about electrical grounding.

The entire body is governed by electricity (and thus magnetism). This is as foundational to the universe as gravity and rotation of the earth. This is core earth science you cannot avoid. It has never been different, and it will never be different. It is a constant. Anyone studying the body would have to accept this, and/or question all their hokey science.

The humanoid is designed to breathe a certain way with the assistance or earthing or grounding to their environment. Modern society and the Western Condition has taken that away. Look you have insulated shoes, synthetic clothes, and you live in a house above the ground with wooden/vinyl/carpet floors. You ride in a car on rubber tires and pass in and out of a host of electrical fields without "grounding". All these induced fields have an effect. Your body as it is insulated off the ground as a sack full of soft metals in an electrolytic solution you become a capacitor/battery combination. You make and store charge without any means to dissipate the charge. If you don't get rid of it, you store it up. Incrementally you become more acidic/toxic, and develop localized pockets of acidosis we call cancer and sickness.

Our recommended approach is designed to quickly and efficiently diffuse the electrical charge and put your body in a situation that it continues to heal for 12+ hours following each session. You continue in a process of reconciliation thus purifying the body electrically, and use repeat treatments to keep things in order. This approach should help 100% of the population past, present and future. Some will have some reactions, because it radically kills off infection and sickness without chemicals. The quick reaction for someone who is sick is a sign of the tremendous power and simplicity in the approach. Astoundingly simple yet powerful. (Go to the website www.TheBrainCan.com for more information.) (Follow-up books will take users to the next level, because there is more!) (We are already developing additional approaches to reconcile finer points in the body. All are about this simple, and powerful.)

The extreme acidosis and low mineralization in many people work against the efforts to properly breathe. As we shall soon see failure to properly breathe increases blood CO_2, which is the real reason for high blood pressure. So many are documented with high blood pressure because in truth high CO_2 in the head/brain is what brings about high blood pressure. When doctors fail to explain this to you, they put you on medication which may not correct this and you have now started a gateway drug to cancer in many situations. (See "The Chemical Conspiracy" of this book for common medical mis-practice.)

As a result of mankind changing the environment faster than the body can adapt we as a culture "short breathe" (The Western Condition). You actually fail routinely and systemically to take in enough oxygen and fail to expel enough CO2 as a result. Since you remain insulated from the earth, you fail to use one of the systems available to you to discharge the excess electrical from your acidic battery pack. By way of culture you slowly build up charge. The charge and acid changes you chemically and your become a seed bed for cancer.

Short breathing in combination with other environmental effects open the door for cancer and "The Western Condition".

Now that you know you have altered the plan/design of breathing, begin taking deep breaths often. Our approach will help clear your lungs and facilitate stronger breathing. Most see instant results and longstanding gains. Amazingly, a host of sicknesses and disease will simply go away with proper, deeper breathing as a result. Amazing, yet simple.

Breathing facts:

1) Virtually everyone you know fails to inhale deeply enough or often enough.

2) Excess CO2 by way of failing to properly breathe brings about acidosis.

3) Acidosis in our blood increases the electrical charge on our battery/capacitor.

4) Too much charge and acidosis leads to cancer by way of acids, electricity, and magnetism.

5) Man's inability to ground out his excess electrical charge causes his concept or signal when/how to breathe to be "off" just a little. We were designed to be better grounded, thus in the original plan we didn't need to breathe as much. (I can explain this further if needed.)

6) Our Acidic Gas Reconciliation plan adjusts the body naturally for induced acidosis and helps offset problems from short breathing.

7) Our Acidic Gas Reconciliation plan adjusts for both low oxygen and high CO2.

8) Our Acidic Gas Reconciliation plan instantly shifts the mineralization status of the body, and as much as doubles oxygenation instantly. It is the only effective means to achieve this.

9) Bottled oxygen or oxygen assist breathing fails to super oxygenate the body, or to flush CO2. Our system can be used in conjunction with bottle/breathe air, and in many cases will completely replace that approach saving the breather much trouble, expense, and embarrassment. (It should save insurance companies MOUNTAINS of money on bottled oxygen and oxygen provision.)

10) Those with breathing or circulation issues will see a radical transformation using our Acid Gas Reconciliation approach.

CHAPTER Fourteen

Renewal Chapter

Virtually all conditions in the body can be rather easily addressed, treated and often cured using a simple, inexpensive, safe, at home approach. (Have you been soaking your feet in baking soda water?) Many health shifts will be addressed in this book and the next book in series. As one can clearly see I feel a simple, safe, at home approach has been kept from society in an effort to finance the lifestyles of others. All pain and sickness can be managed more simply. We will list some benefits to be seen from the approach to follow:

The main problem with Ted Whidden's Emersion system is that it is so powerful (yet simple) that you must control how fast you heal. If you kill off infectious issues too fast your body will react to what is called "Herxheimer's Reaction". This is what happens when you take antibiotics and the doctor tells you that you may get worse before you get better. The Herxheimer reaction comes from a release of toxins when infectious issues are killed. Take Ted Whidden's approach slowly so that your system can adjust to the overwhelming new health shift.

It is clear for anyone to see that CO_2 buildup is a problem with every sickness known to man. There is not a conventional sickness known to man that does not involve CO_2 management and buildup issues within the body. It is a universal problem. It is not introduced to the patient because once the patient understands CO_2 management in the body, then they often lose the dependence on the medical field and pharmaceuticals. People are enslaved by their ignorance.

CO_2 is a byproduct of virtually all cellular respiration and fuel consumption, thus in healthy tissue O_2 moves in, and CO_2 moves out. If/when inflammation or trauma occurs then O_2 flowing in with nutrient rich fluids stalls and stagnates. The O_2 "cooks out" or is consumed with CO_2 as a resultant of that operation. The result is CO_2 buildup. CO_2 buildup blocks oxygen and pain/inflammation follows.

CO_2 buildup blocking oxygen allows anaerobic infection to exist in the body. Once CO_2 is purged, then O_2 naturally comes in, and all anaerobic infectious issues die. By definition anaerobic infection cannot live in the presence of oxygen, thus the majority of all sickness/infection can be removed quickly, safely, efficiently by simply removing CO_2 and ushering O_2.

CO_2 buildup in the body displaces Oxygen in all cases. Clearly CO_2 and O_2 cannot coexist. In any given space of the body there is either an O_2 molecule or a CO_2 molecule, but not both. CO_2 accumulations block the proper oxygenation of the body. CO_2 presence in the body is the cause of virtually every pain or cramp you have had, or ever will have. This principle is core to the function of the universe. It will never change, and has never changed. Since the beginning of time CO_2 accumulation in the body is a sign of sickness. Since CO_2 is a byproduct of cellular respiration it will always be the primary sign of low cellular respiration and poor flow or oxygenation. This has never been different and never will be different. It is foundational to any and all studies of the body.

CO_2 accumulation prevents oxygenation. Forced removal of CO_2 in the body will in ALL situations result in increased O_2 and oxygenation (Given that clean, fresh proper air is available.). CO_2 removal by definition will super oxygenate the body in a normal environment. Pain in the body is a result of poor oxygenation so removal of CO_2 removes almost all pain.

CO_2 buildup blocks healing. O_2 creates healing. Removal of CO_2 is the first and primary step to pain removal and/or healing. Any other step is likely wasteful and deceptive. Oxygenation will cure almost all problems within the body, and true oxygenation can only be achieved by CO_2 removal and/or management.

As body systems are renewed with fresh O_2 one should continue a CO_2 remediation process as consumption and conversion of O_2 results in CO_2. Thus a proper approach to CO_2 reconciliation will be repetitive, and a person could/should expect to see incremental, short and long term benefits.

CO_2 removal and thus oxygenation removes all real pain in the body when one fully understands and applies the process. Removal of pain in many cases will remove the dependency on pain medications which are invariably 60-80% of the problems of many who are sick in today's society. Often removal of pain meds and the use thereof makes solving the patient's real health issue rather easy.

Using this approach prior to any test or surgery would purge the body of inflammation and the foundational components of virtually all infection. Cleaning the body prior to surgery would increase chances of survival, shorten recovery time, reduce scarring, and increase overall success. Ted Whidden's emersion approach cleanses the body naturally, boosts, immune system function, cleanses organs, relieves stress/inflammation, and causes a host of "good" for the body.

Using the approach subsequent to any surgery or procedure would expedite healing, help prevent infection, and reduce scarring.

Use of the approach outlined would greatly reduce all forms of inflammation which would facilitate all functions of the body improving heart issues, brain issues, digestive issues, and a host of issues to be covered in our future books.

Unfortunately the patent system and commercial interests have the vast majority of "science" looking at tiny seemingly insignificant issues in an effort to establish a patent, copyright or some control on a product. Solving cancer, AIDS, and a host of sickness may be very, very simple. The approach we use is simple, universal, and it will work and has always worked. Removing CO2 and toxic gases which are the main and often only blocking agent for Oxygen in the body will solve virtually every condition in the body...........Research groups claiming to be seeking help opportunities for sick people may have misled you all for a very long time. They must change their motives and approaches or risk being singled out for criminal corruption and potentially fraud by misrepresenting material fact and materially concealing information. Clearly there is a line being drawn in the sand. These people have been hiding the simple fact that CO2 remediation would solve many of the natural afflictions of the body. If indeed they were seeking to alleviate problems for the sick, then state the obvious and begin setting people free. Those who oppose this approach or fail to spread the good news are clearly identified as those who would take undue advantage of sick people in society. The corruption must end.

If you started soaking your feet in a baking soda water solution as advised previously then you are already seeing a change. Now begin to work up to where the whole body is immersed. Do it gradually. If you are truly sick it should start killing off some sickness. You may experience some "Herxheimers" reaction as the approach starts winning. (See the website www.TheBrainCan.com for guidance.)

CHAPTER Fifteen

The Cancer Conspiracy

Cancer seems complicated and widespread. That is because it is commercialized. It is not likely complicated at all. We have already demonstrated how to eradicate all pain, inflammation, and sickness. In "The Chemical Conspiracy" book we demonstrate literally dozens of medical mispractice mistakes that are made multiplied thousands of times per day. Are you ready to learn something new?

Most often people with cancer do not die of cancer. The often die of kidney failure, so to sustain the body with cancer we might want to look at alleviating stress on the kidneys correct? Exactly!

Stress on the kidneys as indicated earlier is usually caused by acidosis. Acidosis occurs in the body as a result of low mineralization, and/or attempts to improperly mineralize the body following acidic conditions.

What is the core components of acidosis in the body? You guessed it CO_2 and the acidic/toxin byproduct gases in the system. Ted Whidden's Alkaline Emersion (Acidic Gas Reconciliation) Approach eradicates CO_2 and toxic gases, and sets the body on the fastest path known to mankind for re-mineralization.

Cancer patients often die for one main reason, acidosis affecting the kidney. You will hear of this over and over again, until they embrace a version of the Alkaline Emersion (Acidic Gas Reconciliation) Approach.

The reason in short that acidosis occurs is multi-fold. As we stated previously fungus is often a pre-cursor of cancer. This being known to practitioners they should be telling people that people with fungus are on the track to cancer. Studying fungus a bit further we see that all fungus in the universe requires a roughly neutral environment in which to live. As you will recall the human body is slightly above neutral at pH 7.4. As the body deteriorates it becomes acidic. The more acidic, the closer to neutral, the more fungus, the environment for cancer has been set. Fungus is often a sign of circulation and oxygenation problems.

Here is the key to planting and raising anything in the universe, including cancer. Determine the ideal environment for the growth of an item and develop/maintain that environment. Using the example above the acidic environment is the ideal environment for the cancer. The Western Condition induced by our current environment is the condition conducive to cancer development and growth.

In order to eradicate anything that grows in our environment we would shift the localized or generalized environment outside the area which it thrives. The way to remove/avoid cancer is simply to shift the environment outside that area in which the cancer thrives. Simple really.

Sellers of products want you to ingest things such as raw vegetables, vitamins, supplements, additives, antibiotics, drugs, etc. in large part to control your wallet. They are trying to get you committed to a product line they control. Meanwhile, if they were sincere they would simply show you that one thing and one thing only blocks the worthwhile pursuits of every approach including their own. It is the CO_2 and toxic gases...........A system to remove CO_2 and toxic gases will boost the effect of any and all additives you ever thought could or would do anything.

Acidosis eradication is the issue that virtually every "Alkaline diet", raw foods, health approach is pushing you towards. They are all missing the mark, because the toxic gases are still in the way. They must cobble their system to a CO2 removal/management system for truly sensational gains. Some of their approaches will heal cancers, and sickness nearly instantly WHEN they employ a CO2 removal/management approach. The question is, which was successful? Invariably the CO2 removal is the real super-hero in the mix.

Understanding cancer one will see that cancer is an invading pathogen. It does primarily the same things as fungus, in that it robs the system of resources, blocks resources, and releases neurotoxins. The cancer being pathogenic draws nutrition and blood to the cancer. In the MRI and other chapters I showed how acids create electricity, how electricity creates magnetism, and magnetism draws in the resources to feed cancer. The pathogen consumes nutrition from the body yet as it is a pathogen it has no complete system for excrement and handling of toxins. Toxins build up in the system in and around the area. Slowly the body attempts to reconcile this toxic waste buildup. As it does neurotoxins leak out into the system. Acidosis occurs because the toxins rob, starve, and affect oxygenation of the body. The body begins to decline.

The "fungus" lives and operates within the neurotoxin, anaerobic discharge from the cancer, and creates more neurotoxin. As the neurotoxins accumulate they pushback healthy tissue and consume resources destined for that tissue. In this situation the cancer thrives.

Now, let's look at a healthy body. In a healthy body properly balanced the fungus would not exist, nor develop. Cancer in theory could not begin. (I will discuss why seemingly healthy people get cancer in my Athletic Performance book.)

If the fungus was allowed by some shock/trauma to develop then sickness and cancer can follow. Restoration of proper balance could eradicate the fungus. Same result, no cancer.

If cancer was able in some manner to get a foothold on the body through any means (often by way of neglect) then stepping up the alkaline qualities of the body would empower the body to nourish itself and would oppose the cancerous invader and win. I can explain this or demonstrate it further if needed. Suffice it to say for now that significant reduction of acidosis will remove 80% of all the body's physical concerns in many situations and the body would summarily resist and reject the cancer.

AIDS/HIV and a host of problems are no different. Problem is that commercial interests are focused on small issues to patent/control, rather than the one common denominator of the "Western Condition" which is acidosis backed by high CO2 and toxic gases. Once this is reconciled almost all modern sickness and disease must flee. It is why we focus initially on the removal of issues known to be part of the "Western Condition". You can solve 80% of your problems on your own health wise. The body becomes so efficient that it then begins to address and attack things once thought incurable, such as cancer and a host of misunderstood diagnostics.

Considering the classic approach to cancer using "Chemo" we mistakenly think at times that doctors are trying to kill the cancer. This is not necessarily the case. In the approach to chemo the doctors consider the cancer the weaker organism. They figure the body is more resilient than the cancer. They do not calculate what it would take to kill the cancer. They attempt to figure out how much the body can take and still survive, and then go just short of that. The theory is to nearly kill the body but not completely, and the cancer will pass first. It seems an idiotic approach in many ways. The body is already hampered by cancer.

A better approach would involve building up the body and protecting the body from renal/kidney failure. The body can be strengthened in theory to overcome the same pathogen (cancer). Focus on strengthening the body, and the body will reject the pathogen naturally and starve it out. For a more aggressive cancer approach I will be introducing another set of books to address further progressed, radicalized cancers.

To reverse the curse of cancer all one needs to do is begin shifting the body chemistry. By soaking in an alkaline solution the toxic gases are drawn out of the body. The result is higher mineralization and thus more oxygenation. The buffering that takes place when you soak in an alkaline solution as recommended will use the largest organ in the body (the skin) to remove toxic gas. The body will continue "buffering" the new high mineralized outside of the body. As you continue the body will begin stripping the acid from the region of the cancer. When the acid is drawn down, the electricity is reduced, thus magnetism is reduced, and thus cancer begins to starve. It starves while being pushed against by the body because it no longer has neurotoxin build-up clearing a path for it to grow.

Using the soak method one can actually prevent cancer because the process for initiation and feeding can be prevented.

Interestingly, if you started soaking your feet when I told you then you are already seeing a process at work. Clearly there is a conspiracy or someone would have told you before now.

CHAPTER Sixteen

Common Causes of Acidosis Leading to the Western Condition (and Cancer)

Some of you may be wondering, "How can I test my own pH?" In truth this is very difficult and rather awkward. Processes of the body are ongoing continuously and each organ or area of the body is a little different as a matter of course during their unique operation. The following list contains things that make you acidic. You can make your own list of things that make you alkaline, but for most people that would be a very, very short list, thus making the point that many are more acidic than they should be. During the alkaline soaks your body should "bubble" just a little. The bubbles coming off of you are typically CO_2 and acidic gases so the more you bubble the better. You will note that you bubble for a few minutes and then it slows. At that point you can/should get out allow things to equalized/stabilize and then do it again. You will see action all along, however some only recognize the bubbles after they have done it a few times. It is not that they were not there before, but you may not have known what to look for. Mix your solution to 8.5 pH or until you see bubbles. You should be able to keep and re-use solutions as well. Using a horse trough or kiddie pool we have seen solution hold a good charge for a week or more. The latter days it tends to get a little thick and slimy like. At that time you can see the bubbles better. In short, don't worry about testing yourself. Test your bath/soak water to 8.5 pH, and look for bubbles.

As I give you the common causes to cancer some of you will be disappointed as it develops because your bad habits almost guarantee the success of you getting cancer. This is a result in part of poor environmental engineering and good marketing of bad ideas. You have been sold a bill of goods. We are not exactly trying to condemn all aspects of your lifestyle, but rather making you aware that incrementally you are opening the door and inviting cancer and sickness. What you must understand is the body was originally designed for an environment other than what you live in and for foods and such other than what you eat. The design of your environment has changed faster than your body can adapt. As many of you have ongoing misdirection in your environment you will need to address an ongoing need for adaption or correction. Correcting the problem is not hard. It is actually quite easy, BUT it requires continual correction. Since you continue on the wrong path with the wrong materials and foods, then you will need to continually overcome the problems introduced. Meanwhile, for those with auto-immune disorders, HIV/AIDS, Cancer, Fibromyalgia or any and all other sicknesses they can get instant relief and begin correct the alterations in their body. This will work for men, women, and children and helps explain how they get these sicknesses. We will find that the common core at the center of these problems is the root of all sickness. The system we advocate for correcting it is much like "defragmenting" a hard-drive on a computer. Every now and then things need to be brought back to near original. So look at it as simply "defragmenting" the human body.

Here is a list of what causes or ushers in the condition known as cancer:

1) Improper breathing: Failure to get a good air/oxygen/gas exchange can happen through a host of reasons from poor breathing to a condition such as Cystic Fibrosis or any of many breathing conditions. Not only does poor breathing prevent us from getting the proper air/oxygen we need, but it prevents us from exchanging the toxic gases as a byproduct or respiration. That is why this

entire book focuses on toxic gas reconciliation. Our approach boosts the ability to breathe properly.

2) Energy drinks: Energy drinks are often very acidic. They give you a placebo effect by boosting you with some ingredients such as caffeine while actually increasing acidity of the body, thus lowering oxygen. It is a great marketing scam because you are progressively worse after each one you drink, yet you think you need another one to get the "boost" you need.

3) Soft drinks: Most soft drinks have high CO_2 which you ingest. Your body is already choked with high CO_2 due to poor breathing, so you are over loading an already overloaded system. The phosphoric acid in many cases increases this still further. Much like the "energy drinks" it is a scam that feeds on itself (and you!).

4) Coffee/Tea: For some reason many of these drinks have a cult following, and people manifest demonically when you touch their sacred cows. Meanwhile the tannins in tea and the fermentation process of teas/coffees and acids in these drinks rob the body of minerals. Often I use coffee as an expectorant or for breathing issues, even though it can have a mineral leaching aspect to it. I am not advocating throwing the baby out with the bath water, but you must understand that for each and every coffee or tea you drink then you must counteract the mineral robbing characteristic of the acid. You will note that coffee itself may be the first great energy drink scam. It seemingly lifts the person with caffeine, but the acidosis actually takes them to a lower state, thus requiring more coffee. It is a bit addictive in this way, and in some ways may be one of the gate way drugs to cancer and sickness. If you must drink it, then find a means to compensate for what it is robbing from you. If you haven't or don't then you are missing a part of your body's need for balance.

5) Shoes: Improperly designed shoes prevent mankind from properly diffusing excess power. We have multiple shoe design ideas we are looking to partner with a manufacturer to produce to overcome this.

6) Clothing design: Synthetic clothing serves to "insulate" the wearer. It also prevents a normal exchange with the atmosphere. Charges that would be given off from the skin to help reconcile the body are blocked in part.

7) Skin care products/Cosmetics: Yes, most skin care products are actually designed to keep you buying products. Dermatologists and wacky out of control misguided science applications have people buying and using products that are toxic for their skin. The blocking effect of skin care products prevents the natural exchange at the skin level with the universe. It chokes the body, increases acidosis and thus leads to cancer.

8) Acne Medicines: Most skin care and cleansers use the concept to shift the environment of the skin surface outside the environment where bacteria can live so bacteria is wiped out. Problem is they often use the acidic product approach shifting the body/skin further away from its alkaline roots. In so doing the skin is temporarily clean of bacteria, but the skin must return back through the "sweet spot" for growing bacteria on its way to becoming normal. As it does, the infection returns and they sell more product. Very effective for them, not good for you. Use an alkaline based scrub such as simple baking soda and the skin will be cleaner, alkalinized, and the skin will breathe better, thus killing the bacteria. By the way, shifting the environment in either the alkaline or acid direction will kill the bacteria. You want to shift it to alkaline because you are supposed to be alkaline. You will likely have fewer wrinkles too as the skin will be mineralized. You will heal faster because the skin will be oxygenated.

9) Sun block products: Sun block products prevent the skin from breathing and they layer the skin with oils, acidic products, and thus rob minerals from the body. Meanwhile the cleansing effect of the sun, sea, surf, etc. is blocked, so people are actually getting less stress/acid relief from their vacations and it is leading to more skin problems, acidosis, and leads to cancer (and greater stress).

10) Hand sanitizers/cleansers: Most hand sanitizers used in schools, hospitals, etc. are acidic in nature. They rob minerals from the skin and cause a host of problems. Meanwhile hands are a sensing device the body uses to manage minerals. Notice the astounding increase in rheumatoid arthritis and hand/bone/joint problems. This will be epidemic as generations of students, teachers, nurses, and others grow up using these toxic products. Unfortunately acidic hand sanitizers and toxic approaches remove the softest "trace minerals" first leaving us with harsh minerals like sodium which can cause problems.

11) Shampoos and hair products: In my opinion many (most?) migraines are often caused by hair care approaches and hair care products. It seems natural that women tend to have more migraines than men. This is large part is a result of poor design of hair care, and the marketing of bad products and processes. Check and see. A huge percentage of women with migraines have an "addiction" to hair care products. As we look at the old stereotypical "bleach blonde" and blond jokes, we can see that there seems a recurrent theme in our society of hair care connected with a dense mental state. Many of your products are either oily or designed to "condition" your hair which adds acids to the hair, or the shampoos are "pH balanced" which is a scam for saying they are

acidic. Acidic hair care products make hair shiny and nice in appearance, but the hair on your head is there all day. Coloring products are often excessively alkaline throwing another imbalance. When you coat your head with acidic products, then your head loses minerals in an exchange to balance the environment. As a result you lose mineralization and thus oxygenation in the brain/head. As a result you have headaches. All headaches are the result of absence of oxygen. Oxygen in the body (head) requires minerals. Excess use of products robs the minerals of the body. (This is in part why chemo patients lose their hair. Chemo robs minerals opening the door for sickness. It seems like a real bad plan.) Many people with migraines would see relief by simply shifting to baby shampoo and stopping use of conditioners. (Most migraine sufferers if honest will realize they have an "attack" after a hair care appointment and excessive use of products to recover from the "hair care"). All baby shampoo typically is identified as cheap shampoo with sodium hydroxide (lye) or another alkaline in it designed to lower pH to match that of your eyes. If the pH matches your eyes then it does not burn. The pH of the eyes is much lower than the surface of your body and scalp, so baby shampoo should bring a slightly calming effect to migraine suffers. I will present a number of simple approaches and respond to questions in this regard in our online blog at www.TheBrainCan.com . (In our Concussion Discussion book we will address the migraine, breast cancer, hair products connection. Get that book in the hands of your friends!)

12) Junk foods: Improperly mineralized, over-processed foods create acidic environments, fouls the digestive sys-

tem, and prevents proper absorption and utilization of nutrients and minerals.

13) Microwave use: Virtually all prepackaged food products today use microwave in their preparation and/or packaging. Meanwhile the first and second laws of thermodynamics indicate that heat/energy is not created, rather it exchanges properties. Think of this when you microwave a glass of water, the water heats up but the glass does not. Meanwhile, what changed? The WATER CHANGED! The trace and soft minerals in the water are given up when you use a microwave and the water or food coming from these devices will slowly demineralize the consumer, and lead to acidosis and cancer..........Here is a test for you. Take a large sample of water from any source. Microwave half of it and allow it to cool. Over a period of time water one set of plants in pots with the microwaved water, and one set with the normal water. In only a few days the microwaved water will kill the plants. The other water presumably should not. If it kills plants through low mineralization, then it will kill you!! Do not use it.

14) Toxic water: If these were in order of priority this would be at the top. The use of water that is "relatively acidic" to the body (which means lower than 7.4 pH) is considered toxic over the long haul. As we have pointed out "buffering" occurs both inside and outside the body (refer to Le Chatelier's Principle). Considering the body to be a sack full of minerals and electrolytes, then each time you use water in or around the body with lower pH than the body, then the body loses mineral. It is simple fact. Loss of mineral means acidosis and cancer and a host of sickness is on its way. Most bottled waters are below 7.4 pH and should be avoided. Note: "Purified" or "filtered" water should often be avoided.

15) Reverse Osmosis Water: Reverse Osmosis water is commonly used in and near almost all major metropolitan and coastal cities these day. It allows municipalities to reprocess really poor quality water and send it to their consumers. They strain everything out including salts/minerals. The end result is a highly acidic water product. It will wick the life right out of you. R.O. water is now being sold in bottles in the store for drinking. Understand this water will make you very, very sick. It should be very ineffective at resolving your thirst, and will actually serve to increase heat stroke, dehydration and a host of other short term problems as it leads to longer term problems. Many cancer and fibromyalgia patients will find this is at the core of their sickness. Many mothers and families will find that this can trigger autism in new born babies and a host of problems because the mother is improperly mineralized in large part due to acidic water use. Many people will find their sickness emanates from recommendations of their doctor to drink more water, meanwhile while addressing "quantity" of water, the doctor failed to address "quality" of water, and poor water quality will make you sick every time..... Meanwhile water standards are WRONG! Conventionally what they say is good or sufficient for you is WRONG! Compare the information herein especially in regards to Le Chatelier's principle applied to the body. You MUST get higher alkaline water to heal.

16) Water Treatment/Water Softeners/ Water filters: Common advertisements for water treatment systems and softeners state that they remove "hard" elements from water to include minerals iron, magnesium, calcium, and manganese. For some reason people think this is important. In some instances they market these systems by promising to remove water spots on dishes, glass-

es, etc. The "water spots" are mineral deposits which you would be better off to HAVE mineral deposits in many instances than not. Acidic systems are not as likely to leave a residue as a mineral based system. We have allowed fashion and poor understanding rob us of essential minerals. Often the water treatment approach is to preserve the pipes or to save laundry detergent, but if you are removing the minerals before you use the water either internally or externally then you may be creating a more acidic water thus it is robbing minerals from your body instead of putting metals/minerals in. This is a very good example of concepts in technology gone wrong. It may be one of the largest problems in our society, because too often we tailor our water to suit the pipes or containers we use, and not for our own use. Unfortunately water treatment and a host of approaches remove the softest "trace minerals" first leaving us with harsh minerals like sodium which can cause problems.

17) Drug use: We all can see the before and after "Crystal Meth" photos online. Synthetic drug use employs chemicals that rob or block mineralization of the body. This is why people get skin conditions, their teeth go bad, and a host of other problems. In essence synthetic drug use accelerates the acidosis process. All "normal" "non-drug users" have to do is wait, they are getting the same effect from their energy drinks, junk food, sodas, and the others on this list.

18) Smoking: Many think/believe that smoking causes lung cancer. Why is this? It is simple really. The toxic gases and smoke inhaled creates an acidic environment in the lungs thus degrading the lining of the lungs. The lungs and breathing are at the forefront of the body's fight to overcome acidosis, and fouling the breathing with smoke and toxins slows proper gas exchange. Body cancer

results through acidosis. It often appears as lung cancer, but the whole body is depressed by the process of smoking.

19) Pharmaceutical drugs: Many (most?) pharmaceuticals attempt in unnatural methods to tamper with the balance of chemistry in the body. As an example (Now found in "The Chemical Conspiracy" of this series): we have pointed to "high blood pressure" is actually a problem of CO_2 and toxic gas in the head, and the brain's signal for more oxygen. High blood pressure medicine does not necessarily address the oxygen problem in the brain which is the cause. It addresses issues to slow the system. Tampering with the body chemistry through unnatural means makes blood pressure medicine a "gateway" drug to cancer in some ways.

20) Pain medicines: As we have pointed out "pain" is often merely a sign of inadequate oxygen at the site of the pain. (With an excess of CO_2 in most cases). Since there is low/no flow at the pain site (definition of pain), then taking a pain medicine is by definition not going to reach the low/no flow circulation area where the pain exists. Once we understand this, then we realize it distracts the host from the pain, but allows the low/no circulation area to remain. In so doing the problem actually gets worse, acidosis builds up locally, and once again we have "pain meds" being seen as a "gateway drug" to sickness and cancer, because general condition of the body deteriorates without resolving the problem.

21) Fast Food: Due to poor quality products, packaging, preparation, etc. this is a major source of effective demineralization of the body in that it fails to provide minerals.

22) Housing: Our homes today are full of synthetic products and surfaces. Not only do these surfaces give off improp-

er residues, but they block opportunities to exchange. It is likely that many live in a house made of synthetic products, off the ground, with floor coverings, wall coverings, toxic water, etc. They then wear synthetic clothes and shoes which block them from natural exchange with the environment. In many ways this is how seemingly healthy people get cancer. Runners wear synthetic clothes, then run/train in a toxic environment, and fail to reconcile their systems. There are ways to reconcile this. We look to partner with others to bring products to the market to overcome this problem.

23) Dependence on Gluten free products: Personally we have explored the gluten free epidemic and it appears to be a hoax in many ways. Gluten products are expensive so people make/spend a lot of money. Meanwhile virtually all gluten issues can be wiped out or controlled with a simple approach. Gluten issues appear to really be the signal of digestive lining issues. Often it is caused by some of the products listed above. Meanwhile failure to treat the bacterial infection at the root of a gluten issue allows the problem to continue. This reduces absorption and increases stress. Mal-absorption leads to lower mineralization thus lower oxygen. Noting that most Gluten infectious issues occur in the section of the digestive where serotonin (which counters cortisol/stress hormone) is produced, then problems continue to escalate. We offer simple solutions to treating the illusion/appearance of "Gluten" reaction. Once treated the body can more readily get on track. By avoiding the proper approach to attack the cause, the medical industry is allowing your condition to deteriorate and you become a long time customer.

24) Fiber Food products: Take your favorite "fiber" cereal and add distilled water to it. Mix it up and wait. Test for

pH. You will find wheat "bran", rice "bran", and many of your fiber based food products are significantly acidic. Now review what you have been told over the years by doctors and product purveyors. They have told you to increase "fiber" intake. If they failed to tell you to increase "alkaline fiber" intake then they have mislead you. The increase in "fiber" for the sake of fiber has slowly acidified the systems of millions of Americans. The effect is to break down the digestive system and corrupt the body's natural abilities to heal. This has ushered in the fear/concern of "Gluten Reaction" or "Gluten Allergy". As we have and will continue to demonstrate the fear is a bit of a hoax, yet in combination with all the other product abuse listed here and elsewhere, then "fiber" for the sake of "fiber" may be a very bad idea. What people need are good alkaline laxatives to clean them out because they are full of crap. An alkaline fiber such as green leafy vegetables would be far better than conventional "fiber" options listed above. One thing you must understand is that if you have irritated your digestive tract then it takes 30 days at a minimum to correct the damage in many cases. Your attempts to clean it up using certain "bran" fiber products will potentially work against you. We will find the acidic nature of brans/fibers and the gooey nature of "gluten" help to harbor acidic (bad) digestive bacteria. The alkaline cleanse wipes the area, and shifts the chemistry locally to make it inhospitable for the bacteria leading to the "reaction".

25) Breakfast cereals for children often have "bran" as referenced above. These acidic products slowly erode the immune system of the child. We can see as the conveniences of society increase and use of breakfast cereals increase so does sickness.

26) Probiotics: Ask yourself before someone told you that

you needed "probiotics" where did you get them? You didn't. Where did people 100 years ago and before get theirs? Odds are they didn't. Probiotics often do not work. The probiotic marketing model is to sell you their product long term, so just as others we have seen above, the last thing they want to do is balance your system. If they do, then you won't need their product. Try this instead. Consider digestive enzymes. Often digestive enzymes are found in herbal form. That is the way you and your ancestors were designed to equalize and over-come this imbalance. I often recommend that a person take a rather high dose of digestive enzymes for a while. This will serve to scrub you inside (and out). It is the way things are supposed to be. In "The Chemical Conspiracy" of this book presentation we show you the comparison of "good bacteria" to "bad bacteria". Often they are supposed to be in 80% (good) to 20% (bad) pro-portion. If you get to 70% to 30% then you will be sick. Meanwhile if a business wants to sell you "good" bacteria to balance it out, then thumb your nose at them, and think this way. If you kill off the "bad" bacteria then you are addressing the real problem, and the "good" bacteria will naturally grow in unimpeded. It is much faster, and easier to kill the bad bacteria. (Hint: The bad bacteria prefer an acidic environment! Shifting to an alkaline and a couple of alkaline based laxative flushes could get you back on track or on the way. We will be producing another book very likely on digestive disorders because the commercial interests are leading us so far astray. People need a little common sense approach in this world of chaos and confusion.)

27) Condiments: Look at the condiments you use. Ketchup, Mustard, etc. Look at salad dressings (oil and vinegar). Look at what people do, they try to get their diet right

and get raw vegetables and dunk them in oil and vinegar. Both are acidic. Many condiments that can sit you on the table all the time are so acidic that nothing can live in them. Think about that! They can be served at room temperature because bacteria cannot live in the acid rich environment. Get a clue. That means it is unhealthy for you as well. The super acidic sauces deplete your body of minerals. In many instances the minerals in your salad could be wiped out by the dressing you used on it, leaving you at net negative for minerals from eating the salad. That means your salad could be harmful to your health. Not as harmful as the other things lacking raw, fresh plant minerals, but you get the picture.

28) Processed foods. Virtually any and all processing of foods from the time they are fresh begins to deteriorate their quality and nutrient level. Virtually all forms of canning, preserving, etc. use methods that reduce minerals. The ones that do increase minerals often increase sodium. Often as we have seen with condiments above there are juices used in the preservation stage such as vinegar that are highly acidic. These acids reduce and/or convert the plant ready minerals. In some instances people even drink pickle juice thinking it is medicinal. One thing we may find is the minerals from the original plant that was "pickled" mix with the acid and the acid/vinegar essentially robs from the food. I am not advocating drinking pickle juice, but it does make on wonder what they would get if they just ate more of the raw vegetable that was messed up by pickling.

29) Rain: I have stated a number of times that I am not a huge fan of the concept of "global climate change". As near as I can tell there are a number of liars on each side of the equation. They mislead people for personal or corporate gain. Meanwhile, consider the measureable fact

that there are more greenhouse gases such as CO_2 in the atmosphere. Look around you. Planes, cars, people, etc. It is clear to see. Now here is a measurable test you can perform. Get you a bottle of "phenol" from a swimming pool test kit. Begin testing the rainfall in your area. Invariably you will find that the rain which falls begins acidic. It may or may not become alkaline before the rain stops. Acid rain is falling all over the planet. The rain drops falling is one of the ways that CO_2 and other acidic, toxic gases are cleared from the atmosphere. Meanwhile, as these acid rain drops fall they rob minerals from everything they encounter. This is one reason runners get cancer. They get hot and sweaty and run in acid rain. The body/system is depleted, and they fail to reconcile the situation. Under test if you had been conducting yours long term you would see it takes more and more rain to clear from acid to alkaline. So even breathing the air when rain is falling tends to wick the minerals out of your body as your breathe air becomes more acidic. With more acid rain and longer periods of acid rain, this will help contribute to health issues. Some may recall in years past people would move out to remote desert areas for health reasons. This is part of what they were seeking to get away from...... People go wacky when you mention greenhouse gases, and the concept of "global climate issues". Problem often is they get way out in their speculation of rising oceans and such. All they have to do is teach you to test your rain. On our blog we will instruct you on how to overcome your environment in these and other ways. Meanwhile, stay grounded in your approach to these things. Understand commercial interests will lie to you routinely to sell you something. (Reconciliation of the waters we dump in to the environment by way of removing acids, and re-mineralizing the water will greatly impact the environment in a positive way.)

30) Fried foods: Conventional frying methods uses fats that rob minerals from the food itself. The oils in many instances foul the digestive process, while the food is low mineral, thus a double whammy eating fried.

31) Sodium in products: High sodium serves to displace other ions and minerals within the body such as potassium, magnesium, calcium, etc. The use of sodium to boost pH in water and other such products is misleading because lacking a sufficient balance of minerals leads to irregular body function. Ultimately this can lead to localized (and generalized acidosis) because trace minerals are missing. Be careful with products claiming to be high pH or alkaline because too much of the time they depend on sodium. Sodium is a very highly charged ion product. The characteristics can take over a region and can "push out" soft, trace minerals. Loss of trace minerals as a result of too much sodium and the other de-mineralizing processes is a huge problem. Notice in one of the popular examples of our Alkaline Emersion approach we use baking soda (sodium bicarbonate) as a soak. It is cheap, plentiful, and the sodium ion used OUTSIDE of the body has a strong "pull" on the CO_2 and toxic gases within the body, thus wicks the poisonous gas right out of the body.........Left alone, too much sodium in the body has the opposite effect, in that it "holds" toxic gas in the body. The key in our emersion approach is to create a solution higher in alkalinity than the body, and then immerse the body to wick away the toxic gases. Miracles happen as a result.

32) Stress: Hyper cortisol. Hyper cortisol is known as the "stress hormone". Some might refer to it as the "fight or flight" hormone. Meanwhile, stress jacks up cortisol.

Cortisol tends to alter the body at the chemical/cellular level and replaces good minerals with sodium. The sodium ion build-up in the body can actually attract/hold acidosis in a way as described above. This initiates a form of acidosis and imbalance within the system opening the door for a host of problems. Also, cortisol is opposed by serotonin. Most often the section of the digestive tract affected by the so-called "Gluten reaction" is where serotonin is produced. If the digestive is fouled, and serotonin low, while absorption is low, then you have stress and a host of problems.

33) Epsom Salts: I have seen more joint, nerve and sickness problems frustrated by the improper use/abuse of Epsom Salts than any potentially any other product. Doctors and zealots improperly recommend use of the product even though it is relatively acidic to the body, and thus lowers mineralization. Epsom robs minerals needed for oxygenation and will make you very, very sick.

The Solution for your health is coming!

Now many of you may be thinking that EVERYTHING causes cancer............Well, in essence that may be true. As we pointed out earlier the number 666 in the Bible was the number of MAN! Every aspect of man furthering his advancement and altering the environment is seemingly toxic. Man is the devil himself at times. Anyway, the key is to manage the above products and types of products, while reconciling the body. The problem with developing our environment is man is removing the methods the body has for reconciliation of the acidic condition. This is why we call all sickness today "The Western Condition" because it has been caused by modernization. Our Alkaline Emersion (Toxic Gas Reconciliation) approach will help quickly reconcile this trend and produce instant health improvements with long term gains including eradication of most sicknesses including cancer, Fibromyalgia, arthritis, Lyme disease, diabetes, and a host of problems. It will help to more effectively and efficiently manage conditions such as HIV/AIDS, or things virally transmitted. By removing acids and acidosis conditions, we super mineralize the body and increase oxygenation. It is estimated that up to 80% of all infectious issues in the body die in the presence of oxygen alone and health resumes for many.

Doctors sometimes freak out when you discuss acidosis issues (because they are improperly trained and equipped), meanwhile often they respond that there is a condition of "alkalosis" in which the body has localized or generalized alkaline issues and they can be just as bad. This noted, they are a much smaller slice of the population and in many situations their "alkaline" issue is actually caused by a localized acidosis issue that is blocking a body function. Blocking that function allows for a localized alkalosis, so first thing to treating alkalosis can often be to treat the acidosis triggering it. This is a little complicated so our next book on brains/concussions will address this issue.

CHAPTER Seventeen

The Answer to Cancer

The Solution for your health is here!

Cancer treatment: It has long since been postulated that cancer cannot operate in an oxygenated environment. Meanwhile there may be a simplicity to cancer's existence opening the door for simple eradication. Since cancer is a foreign body within the body it must create a system to draw nutrients within. Under test many have demonstrated that the cancer system feeds and grows aggressively. Critical and rather simplistic to this concept one must recognize that cancer must create a feeding system, yet by the same system of growth it does not have a system for carrying away its refuse. It is not fully integrated into the body of the host, therefore the sewage from cancer's process which consists of de-oxygenated fluids with their life force drawn out of blood resides in the area of the cancer. This produces a low oxygen, acidic environment which in essence protects or allows the cancer to exist. .... It has long since been postulated that cancer exists and resides in areas of low/no oxygen and tends to arrive at old injury areas as a result. Oxygenation could and would likely eradicate the cancer.

Meanwhile, the fecal remains (neurotoxins) from the life process of the cancer is what allows it to live and essentially protects it. The neurotoxins from its life process may actually pave the way of death to the body for cancer to grow. These neurotoxins are in part CO_2 gaseous fluids allowed to remain through the nutrient consumption process. Using alkaline buffering we can "pull off" excess CO2 and acids from the body. This pulling off or "wicking" can be generalized or localized. In so doing the entire body can be super oxygenated. Super oxygenation can likely slow free radical cell growth. Further effects of the oxygenation can effectively shift the environment of the body so that it is healthy for the body, and poisonous to the cancer. In so doing we strengthen the body and weaken the cancer. This approach is substantially out of alignment with the conventional chemo approach to cancer where the body is weakened in attempts to destroy the cancer. Our method can be used to prevent cancer, and address cancer in early/mid/late stages. Whereas not intended for use in a combined approach with the destructive approach of conventional chemo, it could be used in conjunction to make conventional chemo far more effective.

Previously we touched on to how the cancer "feeds" itself. Above we have hinted to a process that cleans up the mess of the cancer, thereby restricting growth. The same process fortunately will help starve the cancer as well. Yes, we starve the feeding process, and remove the waste of the cancer thereby strengthening the body of the host. The body of the host gains the advantage and will reject the cancer.

The feeding process of the cancer works through the acidosis process with soft/medium metals such as "iron" in the fluid. As you may recall from previous discussions the soft metals and acids create a battery or electrical field. The electrical field with residual metals such as iron will create a magnetic field. A magnetic field is what the MRI images. Once we realize there is a magnetic field around the cancer we realize that it uses magnetism to feed itself. Magnetism attracts iron in the body. Iron is in the hemoglobin which is the red blood cells. Now that we know how it feeds itself and how it clears real estate for its existence we simply starve it by changing the chemistry of the body.

The chemistry shift will change the electricity, which will reduce the magnetism, which begins the starvation process. While starving the cancer the same simple process buffers the acidic byproducts of the cancer and in essence attacks the acidity and the cancer itself with highly mineralized (OXYGENATED!) fluids and the cancer dies a natural death. In a healthy body this process keeps the cancer at bay. All we have to do is restore power and oxygenation to the body using a simple solution. Interestingly, our process replicates what "dialysis" does to preserve the kidneys in many ways, and since the kidneys are helped/preserved we increase the quality of life and the life span of the host.

The buffering process is simple. Many of you have already started. Begin slowly. Begin with soaking feet only in a baking soda water solution. The solution should be about 8.5 pH for starters. The largest organ of the body (skin) will be shifted from a relatively acid 6.8 to 7.0 pH to a relatively alkaline of potentially 7.8 pH. This should boost the oxygenation effect of the skin TEN FOLD!!! The body will continue to heal for the next 12 hours as the body "buffers" with the skin. The process continues round after round. Soak at least twice per day, once before you go to bed, and once after you awake. Work up slowly to full body immersion. I would not soak the head just yet. Wait until the body is completely cleaned up. I will address head soaking in my "Concussion Discussion" book. Eventually internal buffering attacks the cancer and destruction begins. (It actually happens rather quickly because cancerous areas will "bubble" under Ted Whidden's Emersion solution as the acid leaves the region.) If a person does not have cancer then regular use of this approach should help prevent it. The key is to remove the blocking agent (CO_2) of the oxygenation process. Removing CO_2 will radically improve every condition mentioned in this book and improve many that are not.

CHAPTER Eighteen

Cancer:
(The Common Denominators of Cancer):

If a person recognized the "common denominators" for cancer, then wouldn't/shouldn't a list be made available to the public? It would seem that the wide array of common issues with Cancer and the aforementioned sicknesses could/should be made public so that people would/could see their behavior and habits are making them a candidate for cancer. Here is a partial list of Cancer's Common Denominators. (Additions to this list will appear in future books in this series.) These are common to the conditions covered under the umbrella of "The Western Condition".

Fungus it seems is the major killer in AIDS/HIV so the process to eradicate the "Western Condition" would serve either conditions.

1) Fungus (The environment for fungus is nearly identical to that required for cancer. Simply shift this environment and eradicate both.)

2) Fungus Exterior Signs (An exterior sign of fungus is the indication of an internal problem 100% of the time. Doctors are failing miserably by not informing and treating people of fungus internally when an external sign is manifest.)

3) Fungus Interior (Fungus does three things in the body. A) Robs resources from the body. B) Blocks resources for the body. C) Releases neurotoxins into the body. .... These three functions plow the ground and prepare the body for cancer. Eradication of fungus should usually be the first step in combatting cancer.

4) Acidosis- Localized or generalized acidosis (Acid condition) of the body is a requirement for cancer to exist and prosper. Alkalinizing the body eradicates the condition for cancer.

5) Body odor- This is often a sign of acidosis in the body. Acidosis is a requirement for cancer.

6) Colored urine- Often a sign of overly acidic urine. If your urine is deep colored, drink more ALKALINE WATER. Not just any water will do. In fact, often water (bottled and municipal) is toxic these days and long term ingestion of water with a pH of 7.4 or lower should be avoided. (See our "rant" on waters in "The Chemical Conspiracy" book.)

7) Smelly urine- Often fishy smelling urine is the sign of infection within the body/kidney area.

8) Infections (Bacteria/Fungal/Protozoa): Infections of all kinds tend to do three things: Rob resources, Block resources, and releases neurotoxins. This dynamic action prepares the "soil" so to speak to grow cancer. The absence of resources, imbalances, and the neurotoxin necrosis (killing) of tissue provides a fertile ground for cancer. Certain conditions of the body are conducive to infections, and the "Western Condition" as set-up by the "Western Environment" is made lethal by commercial interests. Only man does things purposely to destroy themselves and their planet. Many of your modern conveniences are killing you by opening the door for infectious issues.

9) Alkalinizing the body has the effect of increasing oxygen and reducing CO_2 thus eradicating more than half of infectious issues by eliminating the anaerobic infectious issues. (Our CO_2 removal system instantly reconciles this.)

10) Upset Stomach

11) Pain in sides (kidney area) - It may seem/sound rude, or it may be well known to some, but often people do not die of "Cancer". Often cancer patients die from kidney failure. Focus on this, the cancer won't kill you, the kidney shut down will. Kidney shut down often occurs when minerals are depleted from the body as a result of long term acidosis condition. Again, if a person would have stopped their acidic issues, then they would have preserved the kidney, likely preserved life in a manner in which to better survive the cancer. (Doctors will tell you that kidneys balance the alkaline/acid issues within the body. This is an idiotic approach for them to take, because clearly kidney failure and stress is on the rise. Kidneys cannot manufacture minerals in quantity needed, thus kidneys fail.) (Our alkaline emersion approach mimics the same action as kidney dialysis. Preservation of kidney and kidney function is crucial in addressing the "Western Condition".)

12) Headache- Head aches, virtually all headaches are a simple issue. A headache is virtually always sensed at the transition in the brain of oxygenation and lack of oxygenation. Oxygenation of the brain often occurs more effectively in a well mineralized, alkaline body. Again, acidosis is the key/problem. (Our book on the "Concussion Discussion" will discuss this further.)

13) High blood pressure. High blood pressure is really the resultant of low oxygen and high CO_2 in the brain. The brain communicates with the body to increase pressure to alleviate a problem. High blood pressure is the resultant.

14) In the opinion of this author high blood pressure and the medications offered by doctors are often the "gateway" to cancer and other sicknesses.

15) Feet sweat- Sweaty feet and hands are often your body's attempt to expel something. Your body usually expels acidic products (Fecal Matter, Skin oil, CO_2, hair are relatively acidic, and your body is throwing it away.)

There are more things to discuss and present in this regard, but this is a limited venue and we need to move on to begin saving the world. We will return to the cancer issues, digestive disorders, heart repair/issues, cardio/vascular repair, brain/concussion/trauma/stroke recovery, and more. See our other books/offers at www.TheBrainCan.com . We will be in fact eradicating sicknesses simply, safely, efficiently, and naturally at our retreat.

CHAPTER Nineteen

Mass Hysteria

Fighting an existing cancerous "mass" involves so many aspects of life it is hard to address or imagine. Meanwhile setting some of the financial, personal, mental, emotional, and other aspects aside let's take a simple look at the "mass" itself.

If you understand this simple presentation you understand that acid and acidosis suppresses the immune system. Ridding your body of excess acids and acidic gases is crucial to healing no matter how you achieve it. No matter what approach or method you take one must minimize or remove toxic acidity for proper healing to be achieved. This cannot be denied or refuted. Meanwhile, as many of you can attest, there does not seem to be much information on Acidic Gas Reconciliation. This may be the first public release of an approach of this nature, or maybe not?

Under test we have seen where a person can be pronounced whole and complete using modern electronic imaging equipment and the next week the same person is found to be riddled with cysts and cancerous growth/activity. In our earlier example, Whidden saw this happen. We have all heard or seen examples where someone went in for a cancer surgery and the "mass" was much smaller than ever before thought or imaged, or even better yet they return to find nothing whatsoever. This actually happens more than you can imagine. I am not discounting the possibility of miracles, but there is a reasonable answer for cancerous growths and such that sometimes "disappear", or are sufficiently reduced.

Let's focus for a minute on a practical approach for those desperately seeking answers. Let's discuss the person who is moving forward with conventional toxic approaches to cancer (Chemo, radiation, etc.) yet they have a rather large mass, or an "inoperable" mass. This must be challenging for all involved. Let's also consider the "normal" mass or operation that can be greatly reduced in either size, count, or exploration into the body. You must understand that opening the body often invites problems with anaerobic infection, so the less probing and picking that can be done the better. Would you agree?

Okay, the key in part to this approach of Acidic Gas Reconciliation through Alkaline Emersion was developed in part by Whidden's PET/CT scans of February 19 and 26. In one scan he appeared clear. In another scan one week apart he was riddled with cystic problems enough to give concern. There were conditions and environmental effects around both that helped explain what was actually taking place. We were able to prove the appearance of cysts can often be induced.

The images seen as "cysts" in Whidden's PET/CT scan were likely gas pockets or gas effected regions of flesh. A nervous disorder and complications robbed the regions of resources and deterioration set in. The image appeared as a cyst, yet it likely was not. In his case a special condition triggered routine and systematic de-oxygenation of the body. A nervous disorder triggered various twitching/seizure type issues that exhausted worthwhile oxygen in an oxygen depleted system. The result was pockets of toxic gas very likely that fed or triggered spasms, which replicated a whole host of problems, YET to the doctors viewing his records he had cystic issues leading to cancer.............We can now see where ridding the body of Toxic Acidic Gas would make all the difference in the world to this scan/image. (Interestingly left un-treated these toxic regions would have or could have likely developed in to cancer. The best cancer specialists in the region could not/did not recognize this and had no reconciliation approach. By allowing the condition to remain in essence we were "cultivating cancer".)

Deeper discovery shows that the spasms of muscle and tissue in a low oxygen environment can create not only gas pockets, but tissue density issues making the gas pockets resemble growths or issues. It is simple to see. Meanwhile, there are likely countless hundreds (thousands?) of people and potentially millions (billions?) of dollars being spent on worthless chemo/cancer treatments for people who do not have, nor never actually had cancer. We must work on a remediation approach to sort fact from fiction. Very likely our approach outlined here can reduce the size of mass "appearance" by 50%. It can likely reduce the number of perceived cancers by 50%. It can reduce the future of cancer by more than 50% because following a simple reconciliation protocol will prevent many/most cancers from ever taking hold or developing. The cancer industry's response? Will likely be to litigate against us because we cut into their profit margin. Think about it seriously. Review this material closely. It should cost the average customer $1 and low to no risk to help begin their health reconciliation. It will help save 100 million people from a level of pain and suffering in the next few years. It will reduce pain, extend life and quality of life. If the cancer and "health/medical" industry (or government) attack us for bringing you simple truth, then question their motives (and BUY MORE OF OUR BOOKS!).

Following through with Whidden as an example we see that very likely every cancerous mass which is producing or sitting in a pool of acids of its own making has emitted gas which is displacing oxygen and killing tissue. This is much of the discomfort one would feel. Meanwhile a simple implementation of

Toxic Acidic Gas Reconciliation could effectively reduce the perceived size of the mass, clarify the size and location of the mass, clarify the number of masses, eradicate the appearance of some masses, and would serve to clean up/clear up the area making it a stronger survival potential for the host. There appears no down side to the approach, and all positives. Meanwhile, for someone with an apparently "inoperable" situation may see their salvation in actually being able to reduce or "move" the mass simply by more closely and clearly outlining the location and effectively reducing the "inoperable" to an "operable" size. Hallelujah!

As one can see I am not totally against the operation to remove a cancerous mass, but the treatments leading to and from the cancer seem twisted. There is clearly a simpler, better, cleaner, and stronger possibility for approach.

Moving further in the a somewhat radical direction of handling "Mass Hysteria", as many can see and follow the process of acid build-up, leading to electricity, leading to magnetism, leading to feeding cycle, leading to cancer growth and development, then consider the following. Consider a simple "alkaline" injection into the mass. It may require sodium hydroxide (lye), potassium hydroxide (ash), sodium tetra borate (borax), or something as simple as sodium bicarbonate (baking soda), but consider injecting an alkaline into the center of the mass. An alkaline would diffuse the acids. It would greatly slow/stop electricity production. It would greatly reduce magnetism. It would greatly reduce the feeding frenzy of the cancer...........A caustic "burn" inside of a cancer mass cannot be nearly as dangerous as radiation which burns a path through good and bad tissue, or as chemotherapy which is like burning down a house to kill a spider............Imagine the simplicity of installing a simple IV solution to pump weak to medium alkaline into the system to reduce a mass from the center or core of its production.

A key to the alkaline injection concept is to understand that the cancerous cells working in unison seem to operate like hundreds/thousands of tiny capacitors drawing/creating/holding electric power. In unison the electricity produced and thus the magnetism is tremendous. By attacking the center of the mass with a diffusion of the electrical hub is like sending a Navy Seal team into take out a commander of a Terror Cell. The injection in combination with an Alkaline Emersion approach could effectively negate the need some day for radiation, chemo, etc. All the while this approach attacks the cancer and cancer only while making the body/host stronger and stronger and stronger.

Consider this approach in both treatment and reduction, as well as preparation for surgery. Anyone who knows anyone with cancer, or who knows anyone in the field of fighting/treating cancer needs to have this book. We will make this book available at a discount to those who are buying in small quantities to share with their friends, families, and doctors. Share this with your medical professional. They need to know there are options. This book could help coach them through countless healings. Imagine how many could benefit!!

For those in need of mass reduction consider a baking soda/borax poultice applied in the region of the cancer with a stepped up emersion protocol. This can change your situation substantially.

If time is short and things seem desperate and/or you have few options or choices you may wish to consider taking a radical approach to cancer reduction (mass, size, number, etc.). You can likely fulfill the approach outlined here doing it diligently and then have your practitioner image you again. The change will astound you and them. Meanwhile, if demand is high enough we will set up online resources, as well as address it in our blog, as to how to reduce the mass "hysteria". Guide your friends and doctors to this book, our other books, and the website, www.TheBrainCan.com .

CHAPTER Twenty

Treatment Begins

As you begin to move forward you may see/learn something that medical practitioners fail to tell people. Any form of medication you take conventionally can only reach areas where you have circulation. Does that make sense? .... Okay, areas of pain by definition lack circulation and oxygen otherwise there would likely be no pain to begin with. Conventional medications are almost invariably, always ineffective on the actual area of concern. The area of concern due to inflammation and lack of circulation is inaccessible to the medication. Doctors and practitioners should know this. Meanwhile the approach recommended removes inflammation, promotes circulation and for the first time ever allows medication to reach the affected area. Problem is medication is not your answer in many cases at all. All you needed was proper circulation all along in most cases. Taking medication often affects a sensory area, yet often does not improve your real situation. What we are starting with is a process to increase oxygenation and circulation. It is the only real way to create/promote health................. Meanwhile, all these areas of pain are low/no circulation areas. Many of the infection(s) you have are likely anaerobic, meaning they cannot exist in the presence of oxygen. Once we oxygenate the body it will begin to wash and feed these areas properly. Anaerobic issues will begin to die the natural way because we introduced oxygen.............. In the meantime these areas of pain are "harboring" low oxygen infection. As you move forward you will see a series of shifts taking place.................This process is really quite simple and has very little to do with what has happened to you. It has everything to do with how the body functions. Once we get the things that can function normally back to normal, then and only then can you attempt to resolve accident issues. Does this make sense? Contact us through our website and blog for additional guidance: www.TheBrainCan.com .

There are a number of experiences and effects a person will initiate when they start the healing process. We urge all to go to the website www.TheBrainCan.com , engage our blog and other resources for answers and guidance. We have been through what we are guiding you through. We developed and tested the process. Contact us for insights. If you go elsewhere you can/will likely be misguided. See upcoming projects to help with specific guidance.

Okay, at this point there are a few simple (??) concepts we need to address and agree on.

The digestive tract is largely responsible for the immune system, in fact many would say it is 50-60% of the immune system, so it is the best place to start in virtually all situations. Cleaning the digestive system will make everything else work better.

Systems of the body have "buffering" systems to prevent shock to the system. The digestive is no different. An example of this buffering system at work is the use of prune juice as a laxative in the old days. Prune juice is very acidic. Once enough is introduced into the system the body signals that it is better to release this toxin than buffer it, and it opens up a system to dump the prune juice and everything in the pipeline (digestive tract). Does this make sense? Okay, we do not want to use an acidic reaction to elicit this response because at the core of the Western Condition is often too much acid. Meanwhile, adding too much of an alkaline will have largely the same effect and it is a healthier approach.

Introducing an alkaline laxative such as Magnesium Citrate or Magnesium Carbonate has a couple of interesting effects that we want to use. Meanwhile, each kind of laxative recommended by science has often a different process it initiates and cleans a different section of the digestive tract. I recommend a fairly radical approach. I recommend using three different products in sequence. Many will complain about this, but it is most effective and I will share in part why.

First product is magnesium citrate, second is castor oil or mineral oil, and third is garlic (in any form, natural or capsule). These will be followed by very briefly probiotics and enzymes. Each is readily available, taken correctly they are non-toxic and cheap. You should go to the store and get plenty of each of these before we get started. You actually won't need much probiotic. I will explain. You will want to do this again in about a month so get plenty. Women will need to do this three times typically, and men likely at least twice. The products I recommend are cheap and readily available. Our blog will share additional products to use. There is a reason I vary the products and reasons for recommending different ones at different times.

First take the magnesium citrate and let it take its course. This should take 8-12 hours, and can be taken at night with near complete evacuation to occur after waking. Second within a couple of hours of the mag citrate effectiveness passing, take the castor oil. To the amazement of many there will be a response within a couple of hours from this second product, and many will realize the first evacuation was not complete. Clearly the second is still an effective second approach. As soon as the second product clears (which could be a bit volatile), then commence taking the garlic capsules. Garlic is a wonderful thing. It is a natural anti-biotic, anti-fungal, and anti-parasitical. It may produce some fireworks as it helps clean the system, meanwhile if you understand what we have done is we have initiated a virtual sterilization process of the digestive tract. For less than a few pennies (dollars) we have cleaned you from one end to the other. The garlic apparently has low/no side effects, no known toxicity level, and can be taken in abundance for a long period of time. Notice this approach does not give anything in your system time to "adapt" to your new approach. It complete wipes everything out. It is critical to use the laxative approach completely using all three products. You will repeat this because many people have sickness/infection residing in their digestive tract. Also, the digestive tract is the first/best place to start any cleanse. Any time you go to the doctor and they fail to tell you to do this, you have become a customer for the doctor for repeat business. Virtually half of all sickness can be addressed, minimized or remediated using a laxative. Yes, people are full of crap. Change that, and change your world.

In the old days doctors often prescribed enemas or laxatives, but people soon found that the doctor was always going to tell them that, so they would do it before going to the doctor. Most often this solved their problem and thus was bad business for the doctors. They began avoiding this approach and use scare tactics to prevent people from using an approach that worked for hundreds of years before doctoring became such big business. Old school, natural works.

Probiotics are followed to allow the digestive system to be "seeded" with the right kind of bacteria. As a whole I am not a huge fan of conventional probiotic use, because the marketing aim is to create customers. This approach is one that I can advocate. Limited use of probiotics following a laxative cleanse. Do not take probiotics routinely. They are not good for you in my opinion. I will explain on our blog and our digestive series of books.

Following onwards from this most people will see an increase in absorption of nutrients, increase in energy, mental acuity and general increases in performance. This increase is real and can be sustained. Most people will see a decrease in congestion, allergies, cramps, pains, etc. These changes are real as well.

During the process you may likely see a tremendous increase

in mucus production or discharge. Taking a decongestant or expectorant with this process is recommended for many. It will help you clear part of the process that has been blocking your respiration and digestion.

As one can see we have swept clean the digestive tract which manages 50-60% of the immune system. You are already winning in areas where you were not before. Meanwhile the second greatest area of the immune system is the lungs/breathing which could be 20-30% or more of the immune itself. Interestingly flushing with alkaline and garlic will help clear the lungs (expectorant) and we have now "tuned up" the breathing as well, or started that process. You have now cleaned far more than you initially set out to do.

As we cleared the intestines and the lungs we effectively created more "real estate" or area for absorption. The new "real estate" in the lungs gained by expelling mucus allows you to take in far more oxygen and exchange far more gases. This new increased ability to exchange more air/oxygen/CO_2 will create a more painless and possibly pain free life for many. Yes, this can create a pain free situation. Much pain in the body is the result of CO_2 buildup in the tissues. Increasing lung volume allows your body to expel more CO_2 and the result is less pain. It is very simple and very cheap. It is a long standing, well understood, simple concept that will last a long time, and can be repeated as necessary to obtain this position. Meanwhile, it is so cheap and so dependable, that if your doctor told you, then you might not need them anymore, so they simply do not tell you.

Now that digestive and lungs are clearer make effort to supply them with more of the good stuff they need. Good food, typically fresh and green foods, and lots of air. Make a point to inhale very, very deeply now and then. In fact, for some hyperventilation (deep, rapid breaths) will help expel CO_2 and be as effective an approach for pain management as one can find. (Get our upcoming book on "Digestive Issues".)

Now that you have cleaned potentially 80% or more of your immune's defense system there is one simple step. The skin. The skin is likely the "organ" that makes up most of what is left of the immune system. Oddly, we have been misled by science and by product salespeople on how to care for our skin and hair.

When one studies skin or hair they notice that at the very surface where the skin and hair meet on the scalp or wherever the hair is very soft and shiny, so is the skin. Science and fashion have led us to believe this is a healthy condition, however I challenge this misconception. The "balance" which is acidic or oily that most skin products, dermatologists, etc. emulate is a condition the body is expelling. Yes, your body expels the acids/oils to get rid of them. Your body does not want this. Do not emulate this acid/oily condition. Many skin and hair care products do, and thus create more sickness. Conventional cosmetic products may actually do as much to cause the sickness I call the "Western Condition" as eating poorly. Skin products and hair products likely cause as much cancer and sickness as a bad diet.

Imagine that your system is supposed to be alkaline at about 7.4 pH. Your system expels an acid layer (oils) because it does not want it. Imagine as well hair is made up of a high quality protein (keratin) but your body expels that as well. Things your body expels often needs to be let go. Think pooh, pee, etc. Your body expels acidic products. Even your breath is acidic when you expel (sulphuric, CO_2, etc.). All acids need to move away from your body. If/when needed I will reveal how and why your body expels keratin (hair) but it remains attached. Do not worry about this for now.

Conventional products douse your skin and hair with acidic (oil) products to make it smooth like the acidic condition of the surface. If/when these products replicate this and increases the acid/oil then you foul the body's natural cleansing approach. You are actually choking the body, making yourself sick, and thus creating the sickness refer to as the Western Condition............ Now look at your skin/hair products and your processed food and environment. You are adding acid in your food and on your exterior. This being the case, then how can your body create the alkalinity it needs? It cannot, and thus the Western Condition is terminal and it is the root cause of cancer and every known/perceived sickness of the Western Condition.

Nearing the final steps to cleansing the body of toxins is to strip the acid/oil layer. Yes, convention adds more and thus makes you sick. We want to strip this away. Conventional cosmetic and skin care products are killing people it seems. (Get our upcoming book on the "Chemical Conspiracy".) This will cleanse the flow for your body to purge acids/oils faster and better. There will be a tremendous health shift as a result.

In an ideal world a person needs to find something similar to a horse trough or a kiddy pool that holds enough water for complete emersion of the entire body (excluding the head for now. In our book on "The Concussion Discussion" we will cover the head/emersion approach.) Eventually everything will need to be under the water at the same time, yet this should be eased in to. This is a far more powerful approach than it may seem. Just because it looks simple, does not mean it lacks power. It is a method that has been kept from you because it is so cheap, and so effective, that no one can profit from it but you. People will try to discourage you, because they want to keep selling you products. Do not listen. Follow the path of health.

Fill the pool with warm/hot water and add baking soda and/or borax until the pH is about 8.5. In many situations a pool this size will require a cup or maybe 2 cups of baking soda to achieve this. Begin slowly. Soak the feet twice a day for several days. Work up to the whole body. After soaking twice per day for 2-3 weeks, then soak the whole body. Fully immerse the body in it, but do not allow any to get in your eyes. Try to refrain from submerging the head. (We will address head issues in our "Concussion Discussion" book.) Remain submerged for as long as possible. Watch for tiny bubbles. Tiny bubbles will indicate it is working. Every chance you get knock off the tiny bubbles. You will note that new bubbles form. Knock them off too. Every gas bubble you expel is another gas bubble that did not have to go through your lungs or kidneys. Get out and let someone else use the water. Once you are out of the solution for a few minutes get back in. Make sure all along that the pH is above 8.0, and 8.5 is ideal. Add baking soda to keep it in that range. A swimming pool test kit can help you determine pH. (If you expel bubbles it is working. If you do not expel bubbles either you did something wrong or you are looking in the right places. Test your water for pH of 8.5 or above. Try not to use solution approaching 9.0 pH as it may cause a caustic burn.)

Soak in the morning and evening if you can. When you soak try to soak for a few minutes, then get out, and return after 10-15 minutes will boost the effect.

What this dunking or emersion solution does is remove the acidic (7.4 pH or lower) layer from the outside of the body. By raising pH (creating alkaline) the body's exterior will move higher toward 8.5 pH (value of the pool) and thus the entire body will begin ridding itself of acids including CO_2. If you watch and pay attention closely you will see bubbles (tiny bubbles) coming off the body. This is the buffering process. You can/will see pain bubbling away. Pay attention and you will see bubbles where pain and problems exist (Bubble diagnostics!). When the bubbles stop there will be no pain. Amazing. The excess CO_2 and toxic acidic gases are quickly and simply removed from the body thru the skin. Work up to full emersion. It is very important to immerse the entire body at one time if possible. Case in point, if there are any gas, toxicity, pain, or low oxygen areas of a joint, it will clear itself by going right out through the skin. It will go path of least resistance (straight line) out of the body. You must submerge any and all problem areas at a minimum (while keeping the solution out of your eyes.)

As the pain/gases move out of the body, then a virtual syphon will be created in the body. As the gas/poison comes out, it will pull or "wick" oxygen and nutrients into the space it leaves, and thus healing begins.

This process will need to be repeated. As long as you have pain in the body, then you have toxins blocking oxygen. Proper healing cannot therefore take place. Once you get good oxygen and nutrients flowing to an area then pain goes away and great healing can take place. Meanwhile, certain lifestyle and environmental issues will allow the condition to revert time and time again, until the condition is fully resolved. You will continue.

Begin using baby shampoo.

Often a person can/will see about 3 days or so of pain free activity after a session. Some will experience more, some less. Repeating the process seems to give repeated results with a better sense of wellness with each time. In practice I have seen circulation to parts of the body returned after 3 years of partial or full starvation and significant restoration as a result. It is a powerfully simple and cheap process, and seems to be more effective at actually changing the condition of the person than anything else out there. By removing the toxins completely and pulling in the oxygen and nutrition it seems to be completely healthy and free of side effects. A very natural and pure approach it seems.

This simple approach will serve to reconcile toxic acidic gases in the body. Virtually all healing will follow regardless of what condition or diagnosis you believe you have.

The reduction of acidic toxic gas (CO_2) that is pulled straight out the body does not tax the body any longer. It does not have to pass through the kidney or lungs. It has relieved part of the stress of the body. The new oxygen and nutrition to the cell rejuvenates the cells and tissue with the hopes that continued stimulation will rejuvenate the area. The log jam at least is removed for now. The pH of the body will instantly shift and a generalized shift will continue. The acid gas removed from the body will not be there to "flash" a gas or consume mineral. As a result you will obtain and retain more mineral from your next meal. More mineral and nutrition will be delivered to the cell with each successive round of application and meal. The body will get stronger and stronger in a unified approach to wellness.

In the days past before our environment was "adjusted" by modernization you would have been drinking better water, eating fresher foods, wearing different clothes, etc. Our modifications to our world induce this "Western Condition" which is a generalized leading to localized acidosis (or vice versa). This is the design of creation. The same would hold true for all your animals. Strange animal behavior occurs because we cage and contain animals that are better suited to a different environment. Acidosis and its effects are universal and must be overcome. It is really easy to end much of the pain and sickness in this world. Why hasn't anyone told you about this approach prior to now? You do realize that if you immerse in a solution at 8.5 pH (titration level of baking soda) then your body at 7.4 pH or lower will give up its excess toxic gases to the solution? Simple! Anaerobic infection killed through oxygenation. Oxygen and nutrition affected at the cellular level. Radical healing for virtually all conditions. Stay tuned to our books because we are setting an enslaved world free. Share this book.

CHAPTER Twenty-one
Tips and Tricks

There are a host of reactions elicited from following a simple Toxic Acidic Gas Reconciliation. Some folks will get instant relief, some will take longer. Often it is/was a process to foul the system up, so it will be a process to rid the system of problems. Often the "results" from a successful process seem hard to discern by those unaware of what to look for and where to look. In today's world the desire for "instant gratification" will have some searching in the wrong places for the wrong answers/approaches. In this regard we can help.

Our Toxic Acidic Gas Reconciliation plan (also known simply as CO2 Remediation) for the body has been released and explained within this book in part to keep the masses from knowing what simple science may have known for thousands of years. The approach is moronically simplistic, yet likely the most powerful single healing approach in the world. In fact, the approach outlined within this text is responsible for every single healing you have ever had or will ever have. Without these principles you simply cannot heal. Now that you know how to simply manage it, then you can heal as you wish, when you wish, inexpensively, at home. Ask yourself a simple question, WHY HAS THIS BEEN KEPT FROM YOU? If the medical community or government really had an interest to heal you, then why hasn't someone told you before now? I think Someone has, but we failed to listen.

The "health" community has obscured this for a host of reasons in our opinion. There seems to be a conspiracy afoot, in fact in Doc Mathea's book on "Chemical Conspiracy and Medical Mis-practice", we reveal a whole host of additional tips, tricks, and deceptions meant to keep you off the path of wellness........... Further Doc Mathea's original writings on "Unveiling the Grand Conspiracy" goes further in to the root cause for the apparent "fraud" (concealment of material fact) perpetrated on the American public and mankind.

At our website www.TheBrainCan.com and our blog at the site we will be addressing common (and not so common) effects and expectations of the CO2 Remediation approach and others. Very likely there are zealots who wish to respond and defend their reasoning and uses for their acidic products on an already acid loaded body. This is to be expected.

There are physical, psychological, emotional, and other such shifts which can take place with perceptions of new found health, or the perception of the effects of lack thereof.

Within this text we mention things to look for like "bubbles". Well, some of you will make more bubbles than others. Some will make larger bubbles. Some of the conditions with which you use the soak techniques will have bubbles that dissipate to solution not to be seen. Some will see cloudy water. Many of these things can be explained and we will advise further at our website/blog what is taking place.

Physiologically, some will imagine an itch or a twitch, itchy eyes, or any of many "symptoms" as your body begins to correct the chemistry balance of the body. Some of these will be discernable to you. Some will not be. We will explain these further through the website, blog, and other publications as necessary.

Many of you will find someone in your world to refute claims here and elsewhere without foundation. I encourage you to audit their life. Often those who find fault lack solutions. Also, there are people who have elaborately complicated deceptions.

I encourage you to dig deep into their explanations. You will see many who refute simple statements will be misled through other perceptions. We will help guide you through using these and other resources. Unfortunately, we simply can't cover all the possibilities in one book and must close somewhere.

To be totally candid it seems many people are not that perceptive. People have ideas of "right" or "wrong" and in today's society we can see that expectations of the masses really don't always fit with a well-balanced society. Ideas such as universal health care despite reckless lifestyle choices simply does not make that much sense. Why should you be responsible for other's reckless choices? Why should others be responsible for your reckless choices? What we find is that people who have induced their problems through reckless endeavors may or may not have the sense to see the solution. Clearly they failed to properly acknowledge and manage the consequences. Many who read through the list of things that cause acidosis found themselves saying, "I won't quit that!" These are decisions people make. Meanwhile for every unhealthy indulgence there should be some form of compensation otherwise you must accept the condition as it is self-inflicted. Many things such as toxic municipal water systems will take time to correct. In the meantime you may need a reconciliation method to overcome sicknesses induced by way of services.

Meanwhile, for those who wish to see and discuss reconciliation methods such as recommended here, then on our website we will be presenting additional information, product launches, product suggestions, and product presentations with our joint venture partners. (We encourage entities to contact us for joint venture possibilities, and to discover product areas we wish to develop.)

We are presently looking into soap, shampoo, toothpaste alternatives as well as a host of lifestyle products bringing a new level of science to household product design and clothing.

In our upcoming book projects expect to see releases on the following:

1) Concussion, Brain Injury, TBI, PTSD, Mental/brain/cerebral issues.
2) Digestive issues and disorders.
3) Chemical conspiracies and Medical Mis-Practice
4) Oxygen and Athletic performance.
5) Heart issues
6) Shocking concepts of the body
7) Other associated health/cleanse techniques.

Follow our releases at the website www.TheBrainCan.com, our video releases, interviews, and our blog.

CHAPTER Twenty-two

Damascus Experience

In the Bible Paul had an encounter on the road to Damascus (Syria) (Acts Chapter 9). While on the road to Damascus Paul was struck blind. While in Damascus someone who did not agree with Paul (Saul of Tarsus) or his doctrine was sent to him to pray for the removal the "scales" or blinders from his eyes. This book is a Damascus experience for many and I am the one sent to remove the scales of many. Whether you like me or what I stand for or not, the scales or deceptions have been removed. This new truth will open many eyes throughout the world. Some will get it and some will not.

The cells of the body produce a continuous stream of waste from the time of the egg/sperm union at fertilization until well after the death of the person. Cellular growth and decomposition continues consumption of oxygen and glucose until resources are exhausted. The by-product of cellular activity is CO_2. This is foundational to the understanding of basic cellular biology.

If and when an injury or dysfunction occurs there develops a "log jam" in the system with CO_2 and toxic gases in accumulation. By definition functions of the body such as inflammation reaction are designed to prevent a person from bleeding to death. Meanwhile when oxygen rich fluid stops flowing in the body the oxygen cooks out and CO_2/toxic gases are the result. Again the long term accumulation of acidic gas leads to problems. This is basic trauma science. This has never been different and it never will be different.

Inefficiencies within the body which are often environmentally induced allow accumulation of gases. These accumulated gases would quickly be released or discharged from the cell/body if the environment was correct.

Low body pH facilitates accumulation of toxic gases because toxic gases need only be "relatively" acidic to the body to be lethal.

Basic chemistry shows us that opposites attract. Ted Whidden's CO_2 remediation approach simply advocates immersing the body in a solution 8.5-9.0 pH or thereabouts. As the body pH is said to be 7.4pH and virtually all sickness and environmental influences effectively lower pH, then an 8.5pH solution will have a greater "opposing" electron effect than the toxic acidic gas with the body. The CO_2 and toxic acidic gases in the body will bubble straight out of the skin and be released to the solution and/or to atmosphere. This will work 100% of the time. It has worked since the beginning of time and it will work through eternity.

The solution of 8.5 -9.0 pH should not burn the skin or create any adverse effect. The titration level of baking soda is about 8.5pH. This is the main reason baking soda is used. It is not a "baking soda" approach, but more specifically an alkaline approach. Any alkaline above 7.4 pH can/should work. The key is to understand that if you cannot find baking soda, then borax, washing powder, lime, clay, lye, etc. could work. Basically all you must do is maintain pH of your solution in the 8.5pH region. Use the harsher products in moderation. They can all be used to achieve an effect. Baking soda (sodium bicarbonate) has a few inherent safety factors in it, so it is common to find and common to use. (I anticipate radical price shifts upward in baking soda as this approach catches on. Understand the principle and/or follow our postings on the website. We will actually provide an updated set of approaches and combinations very soon in coordination with appropriate product vendors.)

The skin is often called the largest organ in the body. Applying Le Chatelier's Principle to the human body as if the body is a sack of electrolytic solution (which it is) then we see that throughout our day the body (sack of solution) is exchanging ions with the atmosphere through the skin. Ted Whidden's Emersion approach uses this principle FOR us to balance or remediate the condition of the body. The skin and cellular action within the body attempts to balance with the solution during your emersion attempt. The exterior of the body actually changes and "cleans up" or detoxes. When one gets out of the solution the body continues the attempt to balance with the newly balanced skin. In so doing the organs and fluids of the body often give up free gases or toxic acidic waste to the skin. So the process continues well after the soak. Then at the next soak those impurities are further moved out of the body. The process continues from outside working in to cleanse the entire body using a process so simple an 8th grade science student can understand it. As you follow in the process the body steadily gets cleaner and cleaner, and efficiencies improve. This will shift a generalized acid condition in the body very quickly and safely when administered correctly. It will shift a localized acidosis condition such as cancer rapidly as well. When the condition of the body shifts, then often the sickness and condition induced in the body shifts to a healthy condition.

The shift of the body is recognized immediately and it is long lasting. The recommendation to soak before and after bed has an amplified effect to make sleep more restful and productive, while simultaneously making the day healthier. The soak before bed cleans up inefficiencies of the day. The soak after sleeping cleans up inefficiencies during sleep. As this cycle is continued most will see significant bodily improvement in 3-7 days.

For many with Lyme disease or other major anaerobic infectious issues you will see a very powerful shift. Some will see a "Herxheimers" reaction because this is so powerful. This is not to be feared. It is to be embraced because for less than $1 you are finally winning. We will be providing guidance to those with such reaction through our blog, website, and other resources. For many, if you are not Herxing, then the sickness is winning. Press through.

The evidence of solution working is absolute, manifest power demonstrated by bubbles exiting the skin. These bubbles are gases released through the above process. Clearly your body did not need these gases. Clearly oxygenation increases, inflammation decreases, pain decreases, life increases, and health restoration is initiated.

Understand that the bubbles that come out of the body were toxic gas that your body no longer has to deal with. This is powerful because this boost kidney and lung function immediately. This produces an immediate efficiency and boost to immune function. The process actually replicates much of what kidney dialysis does, so for the cancer patient this can extend life of the kidney and quality of life. The kidney "machine" works similar, but they run what appears a risky removal of fluids from the body for a similar removal. Dialysis is in some ways like MRI. The concept and operation to design, develop, and build the machine shows they knew all along how to reconcile/remediate toxic gases within the blood, but if they told you they wouldn't make as much money. It is time to shift the wealth of the wicked and teach your friends and family how to clean up their blood, tissues, organs, cells, and body. Alkaline Emersion to the rescue!

The cellular process which produces cellular waste gases is continuous. For this reason an alkaline immersion regime need be established until the body's processes are fully reconciled. As one continues to function in a poorly reconciled environment they will need to continue. This is why we refer to is as CO2 remediation.

This will work. This process has been hidden from you for a host of reasons. It has been hidden from others as well. You owe it to your friends, family, and associates to provide them a copy of this book. Yes, you are your brother's keeper.

A veritable conspiracy would have to be in place to have hidden this from you. Oppose the conspiracy. Spread the word!

The "Western Condition" is a resultant in part of the dietary and environmental factors leading to toxic acidic gas accumulation (CO2) within the cells, tissue and body. Cancer and most other sickness depend on toxic gas accumulation in one way, shape, or form.

The "Simple Solution for the Western Condition" is to employ alkaline immersion (a "solution") for remediation of temporary and ongoing conditions.

There is no process more basic to body health than expressed within this book. It is foundational to cellular, tissue, and body function. How is it that it has been obscured from humanity? Those who have obscured it for their own gain have likely obscured other things. See our future releases to conquer more the mystery and misery.

It is time for all the scales and blinders to come off. Begin setting captives free. Share this book.

CHAPTER Twenty-three

Revelation: *The Great Healer*

Some may consider my approach "alternative medicine", but it is not. In order to lump a process into a category we need to understand what the term "alternative" means.

As we look at the modern commercial approach to medicine we should consider THAT approach to be "alternative" because to this point in history we never had it. The vast majority of medicines on the market today were not available 20-50 years ago, so the modern "snake oil" approach to medicine appears the alternative. The use of the population as guinea pigs has served to obscure better, safer, more reliable old age approaches.

Previously I advised that we are not practicing medicine because this indicates an interest in sickness and other undesirable issues. We are practicing chemistry that is as old as time itself. Some may refer to me as an "Alchemist". Well, in some ways this is an endearing term. In others, maybe not so. Our research has been connected to a wide host of exploration in to the unknown, yet when you consider that practicing health, an herbal approach, or an alkaline emersion design is alternative, consider this:

1) Nebuchadnezzar: In the Book of Daniel in the Bible, he was afflicted by a condition that drove him into a nervous disorder and a mental condition. He was restored using grasses of the field.
   Daniel_5:21 And he was driven from the sons of men; and his heart was made like the beasts, and his dwelling was

with the wild asses: they fed him with grass like oxen, and his body was wet with the dew of heaven; till he knew that the most high God ruled in the kingdom of men, and that he appointeth over it whomsoever he will.

2) Naaman: In the Book of Second Kings (Kings II) of the Bible, Naaman was instructed by the Prophet Elisha to go dunk seven times in the Jordan River. For your information the phase of the Jordan when and where he was instructed was a muddy alkaline river. The mud/alkaline from the river would have remained on his skin following the dunking and it would continue to dry and heal his sores by way of super oxygenation. The Jewish faith has a concept called the Mikvah or "Living Waters". The repetition and the process of cleansing of the body of sickness is nearly the exact same as prescribed. This is not alternative medicine, this is traditional medicine being resurrected:

2 Kings 5:9 So Naaman came with his horses and with his chariot, and stood at the door of the house of Elisha.

2 Kings 5:10 And Elisha sent a messenger unto him, saying, Go and wash in Jordan seven times, and thy flesh shall come again to thee, and thou shalt be clean.

3) John/Jesus, Healing of the Blind: In the Book of John of the Bible John tells us a story of Jesus healing a blind man. Jesus takes clay (calcium powder and an alkaline) and spits in it (and alkaline fluid from the body), and makes a paste to heal a blind man's eyes, and then tells him to clean in the pool of Siloam. This is EXACTLY THE SAME approach/cure represented using a poultice of alkaline on the eyes. The clay/spittle acts as a "poultice" local to the sick area of the body to remove a localized acidosis. This is highly recommended in conjunction with many localized illnesses. We too use a poultice as you have seen. The person is then told to wash in the pool of

Siloam which in essence would remediate the generalized acidosis condition. A "Mikvah" so to speak.

John 9:6 when he had thus spoken, he spat on the ground, and made clay of the spittle, and he anointed the eyes of the blind man with the clay,

John 9:7 And said unto him, Go, wash in the pool of Siloam, (which is by interpretation, Sent.) He went his way therefore, and washed, and came seeing.

Note: In this instance the use of "spittle". Many of you have seen our reference to using "baby shampoo" to wash with because it is balanced to match the pH of the eyes, hence "No more tears." Meanwhile, many of you have seen someone take a contact out of their eye, "wash" it in their mouth and put it back in. This gives indication that saliva is relatively close in pH to that in our mouth, otherwise the contact would burn when put back in the eye. Now, we see Jesus takes a presumably calcium/magnesium based clay, mixes it with a high pH solution (spit) and puts in in the eyes, then tells him to wash. This is EXACTLY THE SAME healing we prescribe.

4) In relation to the saliva/pH example above we also see in Luke's Book in the Bible wherein it states:

Luke 16:20 And there was a certain beggar named Lazarus, which was laid at his gate, full of sores,

Luke 16:21 And desiring to be fed with the crumbs which fell from the rich man's table: moreover the dogs came and licked his sores.

Even animals, dogs, and the ancients knew that alkaline use of saliva and such on wounds would produce a healing or cleansing.

5) John Chapter 5, of the Bible states the following:

John 5:1 After this there was a feast of the Jews; and Jesus went up to Jerusalem.

John 5:2 Now there is at Jerusalem by the sheep market a pool, which is called in the Hebrew tongue Bethesda, having five porches.

John 5:3 In these lay a great multitude of impotent folk, of blind, halt, withered, waiting for the moving of the water.

John 5:4 For an angel went down at a certain season into the pool, and troubled the water: whosoever then first after the troubling of the water stepped in was made whole of whatsoever disease he had.

John 5:5 And a certain man was there, which had an infirmity thirty and eight years.

John 5:6 When Jesus saw him lie, and knew that he had been now a long time in that case, he saith unto him, Wilt thou be made whole?

John 5:7 The impotent man answered him, Sir, I have no man, when the water is troubled, to put me into the pool: but while I am coming, another steppeth down before me.

John 5:8 Jesus saith unto him, Rise, take up thy bed, and walk.

John 5:9 And immediately the man was made whole, and took up his bed, and walked: and on the same day was the sabbath.

Meanwhile, what so many fail to see in this passage is that the pool of Bethesda was believed to be healing BEFORE the prophets arrived! Read it again! The problem was that the paralytic could not get there fast enough. Meanwhile, when we research this closely we find a mine nearby for "sodium tetra borite" (Borax!). A fissure in the ground that would percolate a borax solution into the pool now and then would create a disturbance (angel's wing) and the next person in the pool would be healed from the alkaline emersion release into the pool, and thus they would "buffer" with the pool, lose excess toxic acids/CO2, thus producing healing...........The healing of the pool is EXACTLY what we are advocating in this book. It is traditional chemistry to treat ailments of the Body. The alkaline "percolation" serves to remove the excess acidosis from the body. It has always worked and it always will.

The Pool of Bethesda was a Mikvah or "Gathered Living Water". Jesus by healing the paralytic was making an inference to "Living Water" referred to elsewhere.

The teaching released in this book is as old as the world itself. It is the plan of the Creator for reconciling health in the body. It has been the only thing very likely that has ever healed you of anything, yet you were likely unaware of what was taking place or how to better manage it. By becoming more aware and more vigilant you can create the healing of the ages. Furthermore, deeper endeavors into the Book of the Bible for educational study may be able to heal other ailments you may have. There are great secrets hidden in plain view in the Bible waiting for you to discover the healing for cancer and all other ailments of the human condition. Unfortunately, our culture in decay is missing out in large part due to a decline in health, culture and society known as the decline of "The Western Condition". (See Doc Mathea's book of "Unveiling the Grand Conspiracy" to learn more.)

What our society and culture may see in this process is a form of "Baptism", but not specifically that, but actually more akin to the "Mikvah" of the Jewish culture which requires cleansing with natural waters. The practice of "Baptism" is actually a type/style of Mikvah, however traditions of men have often corrupted the practice. (Baptism is a type of Mikvah in many ways, but Mikvah is not necessarily Baptism. Mikvah is a regular ceremonial cleansing. Baptism is/was this ceremonial cleansing in theory. At issue is the need for long term, regular cleansing as was practiced in Mikvah.) God gave His people methods to balance with their environment to overcome the traditions of men indicating the Mikvah has taken place for thousands of years. Oddly, the practice and "rules" have been kept secret and today the rhyme and reason for Mikvah are somewhat obscured. We see today the practice of using filtered water may be keeping some in the Jewish faith from getting all they can from the Mikvah. The original "gathered living waters" were actually pure. Today they are not a result of industrialization and pollution.

The use of baking soda or borax in the Mikvah would greatly aid in the intended healing/cleansing. The original "gatherings of waters" were far more mineralized than our waters today. By way of industrialization and population increases we have demineralized waters where they are gathered. We see in this book there is practical application for this approach, and arguably a separation of man from his roots have taken place by failing to follow the Mikvah origins. Digging deeper the use of the "Pool of Siloam" and the "Pool of Bethesda" (and the Jordan River for that matter) were "Mikvah" used by Jesus and the prophet Elisha. John the Baptist used deep waters to in theory fully immerse people at baptism. The relative obscure nature and approach to Mikvah by the Jewish population has likely increased certain risks of cancer (use of tainted waters and rain water/acid rain in highly populated regions), meanwhile it is easy to see the plan for purification of the body of acidosis and thus likely the cure for cancer was given to these people long before it was needed. What we will find is those groups or areas where they have the Mikvah right or closer to right will have a lower incidence of cancer. Where they have it wrong, there will be a higher incidence. This is environmentally induced as improperly balanced water (relatively acidic) would make the person sicker, not healthier. Proper implementation of Mikvah is simply an astounding extension of God's outreach to all people. The study of this long abandoned or distorted convention they call Mikvah can set mankind free.

Traditions of man often corrupt good things. Something once thought to be a "ritual" cleanse actually has/had a practical and medical use. Somehow this is/was obscured in history, and is clearly something needed in today's society. This will be further explained as well as benefits to pregnancy, unborn, new born babies, autism research, and breast cancer in "The Chemical Conspiracy" of this series.)(Make sure your Mikvah is strong alkaline waters as were gathered at the time of Creation (Genesis), and your Mikvah will begin to transform the people. Clearly due to industrialization and such rain water lacks mineral today and contains acids you do not need.) (If Alkaline Mikvah was implemented at the Cystic Fibrosis centers, burn centers, wound care centers, hospitals, and all forms of care facilities then radical transformations would begin to take place.)(Interestingly there is a dynamic that takes place in a larger set of interconnected pools as indicated previously in this book. At 200 gallons a radical transformation takes place. I will explain that further in future writings. Interestingly we discovered this transformation before we connected our approach/discovery to the origins of Mikvah.)

As you may note, we began with soaking/washing the feet. Ancient tradition began there. There is a clear and simple science (and spiritual?) reference to begin by washing feet. As the feet are the furthest thing from the core of the body and operational organs, and as they are traditionally the "lowest" the heavier specific gravity "acids" often occur there. We know that, as did Jesus. (Whether you consider Jesus a Rabbi, a Prophet, a Man, or Messiah, you must acknowledge use of healing waters and "mikvah" as outlined some 2000 years ago.) It is often the best place to start with the cleanse leading to full emersion in a solution (as we see above at the Pool of Siloam and the Pool of Bethesda, Mikvah). Start slowly and work up as transformation can be radical.

Those who are ill or believe to be ill will see greatest benefit if they immerse before and after sleep (in the night before bed and in the morning after sleep) and leave the 8.5 pH solution on their skin as long as possible. It is not recommended to wash it off. Do this for one week to one month consistently noting any and all changes. (Contact us to advise us of your progress.) The shift in removal of excess toxic acidic gases (Toxic Gas Reconciliation) will be a process. Incrementally the body will shift to a more natural condition. Some shifts will be immediate. Others will take time. It is somewhat like Elisha and Naaman's encounter. It seems simple, but it is very powerful and will work on a host of things which you and your doctor may be unaware. In so reconciling the body the body will actually enjoy excess resources to take care of the core issue (cause) of whatever makes you ill. It will work miracles for many. Get moving in the right direction and report back to us on your progress. We will guide you further.

Get on a path to wellness. I say to you, "Pick up your mat and walk!"

Get healed. Get whole. Get set free. The Plan of God, is the plan of good.

This is not **"The End"**, but rather this is **your "New Beginning"**. Return to **"In the beginning"** and share that message with others. Bless you and yours.

Interestingly the "Answer to Cancer" in many ways has been hidden in plain view since before "cancer" was "discovered" by modern science. The best form of treatment/cure may have been hidden in a book called the BIBLE which science and other lost souls have been trying to keep you from reading. I often wonder what else you might find, and you can only imagine what else I have found. Stay tuned, there is more rebel revelation coming soon!

The "Simple Solution to the Western Condition" was implemented and demonstrated in the "Mikvah" long before it was needed 2000+ years ago. It worked then, and it will work today and always. Arguably no other approach will have as universal an appeal or such an effective response. Hidden in plain view for all to see for over 2000 years. Imagine what you may be missing.......

If you are offended by the use of Biblical Scripture in closing this presentation, imagine what else you and others might be missing from the Text by not properly reading it and applying its principles to our lives. Imagine those "men of science" who have said the Bible had no meaning in your life. They were clearly wrong in their medical approaches and ideologies. They were clearly wrong similarly in the irrelevance of the Biblical Text. There are a multitude of healings of all kind hidden in plain view for the world to see, if they would dig into the Book. There is more to come.

Consider this as well, thousands of preachers/teachers scour the pages of the Text weekly in effort to bring a real world application to life in a 2000-3000 year old set of Texts. If they only dug deeper and differently cancer may have never got a foothold to begin with. The Bible refers to the "Traditions of Men" which make the "Word of God" of none effect. Maybe it is time we revisit the Scriptures with a view to learning how to use it more effectively?

Clearly immersion is not "new". Clearly it is not "alternative". Clearly it was given at the beginning of time and it is being restored as promised. Knowledge in and of the earth is being restored as promised.

Daniel 12:4 But thou, O Daniel, shut up the words, and seal

the book, even to the time of the end: many shall run to and fro, and knowledge shall be increased.

There is much more to come for you and yours as our staff prays regularly for those who read this book. You do know we pray for you, don't you? Do you want to know what we pray? Super! I want you to know what we pray so that when you see it, then you know where it came from. We pray that those who read this book will be given the ABSOLUTE, UNDENIABLE, MANIFEST POWER and PRESENCE of GOD in their lives. Watch as God moves through your day and the day of others. Report back to us to tell us your story. Hundreds (Hundreds of thousands?) will be healed!

In our "Concussion Discussion" coming in this book series we will use these principles and more in a modified approach to end much mental pain, suffering, torment, neurological issues, and problems. Do not miss that book. Share this with those who may be in need of healing in that area, because this may be the first step for many to returning to their full health following head injury.

At times throughout this book you likely thought of yourself and others who could use healing. Now, stop and think of ten (10) friends and/or family members. Go to the website and order a bulk shipment of 10+ books to distribute to those you love and care about. We will provide substantial discount to you for your efforts to heal your friends and family. We want to reach 100 million people as fast as possible. Will you come alongside of us for the super-hero effort? www.TheBrainCan.com

This book is in many ways the initiation of a bridge from where we are to where we should be. It should be read and embraced by all those seeking health for themselves or others. It is not meant to be offensive, however there are things that may offend. Education is often that way. People often are excited on their first level of revelation, skeptical on their second level, and cynical on their third. It will take time for some to see the simplicity in the many messages obscured by present day (corrupted) approaches. Share this book with a friend. Their health and healing may depend on it. Our website www.TheBrainCan.com can provide more resources and information.

Areas to consider for use of
Ted Whidden's Alkaline Emersion
(Acidic Gas Reconciliation) Approach.
Stay tuned to our website and blog
for additional resources and approaches.

Emersion/Electrolytic Applications/Potential:

- Kidney support, dialysis, field dialysis
- Organ transplant support
- Cancer maintenance, treatment, process leading to cure (?)
- Pre-cancer treatment
- Post Cancer treatment
- Breast Cancer preventative treatment
- Pre-Pregnancy, Post Pregnancy, During Pregnancy: To boost new born survival, clean-up, and preparation for new life on earth
- Early childhood cleaning, maintenance, cure of fungus and other issues
- Newborn and Premature birth development and preparation (Note: Many have seen the posts online regarding the twins babies in which one was sick as they were separated. A nurse allegedly put the babies together and the sick child regained strength. There is/was a shift that can be demonstrated and tested. That shift can be replicated using the emersion approach, especially when there isn't a "twin"

to share the burden of the sickness. We will write more on this later.)

- Woman care:
PMS, Morning Sickness, Pre Menopausal, Menopausal, Post-Menopausal
- Wound care, Burn care, Pain Relief:
- Life/Gas Maintenance: Gangrene, Infectious Issues remediation:
- Super Circulation/Oxygenation:
- Pre-Surgery/Post Surgery: Use of the Alkaline Emersion (Acidic Gas Reconciliation) approach prepares the body for surgery by lowering toxic gases and increasing oxygenation. Healing will be accelerated, noting a proper Alkaline Emersion (Acidic Gas Reconciliation) exists at a high, alkaline pH in which bacteria cannot survive. By shifting the body generally in the alkaline direction total healing was well as localized healing occurs reducing time for recovery and scarring.
- Medical pre-operation preparation, Post operation in medical environment, Pre-hospitalization/Post-hospitalization
- Diver Recovery: Alkaline Emersion (Acidic Gas Reconciliation) is a very effective way of removing many of the toxic gas buildups from diving under pressure.
- Pre-Hyperbaric treatment:
- Lyme Treatment: Lyme disease (See future write-up on quick, simple, easy way to eradicate Lyme.)
- Trauma treatment
- To enhance Chiropractic care, To en-

hance/facilitate massage care and manipulation/therapies
- Anti-inflammation
- On treatment (cure?) of anaerobic bacteria/infection
- Treatment of fungal infection (bacteria/fungus/protozoa)
- Alkaline vs. Acid Antibacterial:
- Anaerobic infections:
- Asthma, COPD, Cystic Fibrosis, Allergies, breathing difficulties
- Fever control (Removal of Insulating gases) (Fever reduction with a twist):
- Cancer: (The answer to cancer?)
- Shingles, Herpes and other such outbreak management
- Heat stroke (OSHA?)
- Cramps, Gout, Diabetes
- To overcome induced problems from Hair/skin products recommended by dermatologists:
- Breathing Issues such as asthma, COPD, etc. (Clear CO_2)
- CO_2/Gluten connection
- Diabetic Circulation issues
- Drug recovery/rehab: Helps to remineralize the body, stabilize systems and ease drug withdrawals.
- Heart Attack/Stroke: (See our book on the Concussion Discussion)
- Mental conditions   (See our book on the Concussion Discussion)
- Stroke (See our book on the Concussion Discussion)

- Epilepsy (See our book on the Concussion Discussion)
- Alzheimer's (See our book on the Concussion Discussion)
- Sundowners: (See our book on the Concussion Discussion)
- Full Moon affect (Infectious issues)
- Bipolar Issues (brain/mental toxins) (See our book on the Concussion Discussion)
- Mental issues (See our book on the Concussion Discussion)
- Sleep disorders (See our book on the Concussion Discussion)
- Migraines (See our book on the Concussion Discussion)
- Mental Health: (See our book on the Concussion Discussion)
- Overcoming Oxygen deprivation issues (Head/Brain/Body/Organs) (See our book on the Concussion Discussion)
- Concussions/Traumatic brain injury (See our book on the Concussion Discussion)
- Hangover recovery (See our book on the Concussion Discussion)
- Oxygen Deprivation issues Body, Organ, and Head/Brain
- Brain work/ Cerebral/Mind enhancement
- Any/All breathing lung conditions, Any/All joint conditions, Any/All muscle conditions, Any/All organ conditions, Any/All skin conditions
- CO_2 removal to maintain the "garden" conditions of the body. Eradicating the CO_2 build up removes

the possibility of accumulation leading to bodily sickness.

- Anti-aging (as acid and acidosis is responsible for most aspects of aging)
- Athletic performance enhancement and recovery
- Athletic/Physical Performance=> pH Affects oxygen => oxygen affects endurance
- Oxygenation/Sexual performance
- Athletic performance: We are soon to release an additional book called, "Oxygen for Athletes". Athletic recovery following performance or preparation for competition could be helpful.

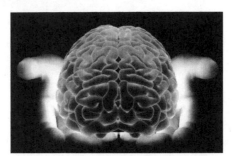

Stay Tuned for my Next Blockbuster!!

A Block buster "literally" as we release the book,

"The Concussion Discussion:
TheBrainCan Recover".

Ted Whidden's condition as referred to within this book stemmed in part from severe concussion, TBI, PTSD, and related issues that spun hormones out of control. What we demonstrate is there is a fabric of interwoven issues that need to be peeled off in a specific way in a specific order. Using the "Answer to Cancer" as a foundation we present a revolutionary set of processes to clean up cerebral problems of all kinds.

As you will soon see,

TheBrainCan recover!
TheBrainCan be restored!
TheBrainCan be re-started!